CHURCH:

WHY BOTHER?

Resources by Philip Yancey

The Jesus I Never Knew

What's So Amazing About Grace?

The Bible Jesus Read

Reaching for the Invisible God

Where Is God When It Hurts?

Disappointment with God

The Student Bible, General Edition (with Tim Stafford)

Meet the Bible (with Brenda Quinn)

Church: Why Bother?

Finding God in Unexpected Places

I Was Just Wondering

Soul Survivor

Rumors of Another World

Prayer

A Skeptic's Guide to Faith

Grace Notes

Vanishing Grace

Books by Philip Yancey and Dr. Paul Brand

Fearfully and Wonderfully Made

In His Image

The Gift of Pain

In the Likeness of God

PHILIP YANCEY

CHURCH:
WHY BOTHER?

ZONDERVAN

Church: Why Bother?
Copyright © 1998 by Philip D. Yancey

This title is also available as a Zondervan ebook.
Visit www.zondervan.com/ebooks.

This title is also available in a Zondervan audio edition.
Visit www.zondervan.fm.

Requests for information should be addressed to:

Zondervan, 3900 *Sparks Dr. SE, Grand Rapids, Michigan 49546*

This edition: ISBN 978-0-310-34440-7 (softcover)

Library of Congress Cataloging-in-Publication Data

Yancey, Philip.
      Church, why bother? : my personal pilgrimage / Philip Yancey.
         p. cm.
      ISBN 978-0-310-202004 (hardcover)
      1. Church. 2. Yancey, Philip. 3. Church attendance. I. Title.
    BV600.2.Y18 1998
    262—DC21   96-00000

All Scripture quotations, unless otherwise indicated, are taken from the Holy Bible: New International Version®, NIV®. Copyright © 1973, 1978, 1984, 2011 by Biblica, Inc.® Used by permission. All rights reserved worldwide.

Published in association with the literary agency of Alive Communications, Inc., 7680 Goddard Street, Suite 200, Colorado Springs, CO 80920. www.alivecommunications .com

First printing July 2015 / Printed in the United States of America

CONTENTS

FOREWORD
BY EUGENE H. PETERSON

A favorite story in our home as our children were growing up was of John Muir at the top of the Douglas fir in the storm.* Whenever we were assaulted by thunder and lightning, rain sluicing out of the sky, and the five of us, parents and three children, huddled together on the porch enjoying the dangerous fireworks from our safe ringside seat, one of the kids would say, "Tell us the John Muir story, Daddy!" And I'd tell it again.

In the last half of the nineteenth century, John Muir was our most intrepid and worshipful explorer of the western extremities of our North American continent. For decades he tramped up and down through our God-created wonders, from the California Sierras to the Alaskan glaciers, observing, reporting, praising, and experiencing—entering into whatever he found with childlike delight and mature reverence.

At one period during this time (the year was 1874) Muir visited a friend who had a cabin, snug in a valley of one of the tributaries of the Yuba River in the Sierra Mountains—a place from which to venture into the wilderness and then return for a comforting cup of tea.

One December day a storm moved in from the Pacific—a fierce storm that bent the junipers and pines, the madronas and fir trees as if they were so many blades

---

*Edwin Way Teale, ed. *The Wilderness World of John Muir* (Boston: Houghton Mifflin, 1954), 181–90.

of grass. It was for just such times this cabin had been built: cozy protection from the harsh elements. We easily imagine Muir and his host safe and secure in his tightly caulked cabin, a fire blazing against the cruel assault of the elements, wrapped in sheepskins, Muir meditatively rendering the wildness into his elegant prose. But our imaginations, not trained to cope with Muir, betray us. For Muir, instead of retreating to the coziness of the cabin, pulling the door tight, and throwing another stick of wood on the fire, strode *out* of the cabin into the storm, climbed a high ridge, picked a giant Douglas fir as the best perch for experiencing the kaleidoscope of color and sound, scent and motion, scrambled his way to the top, and rode out the storm, lashed by the wind, holding on for dear life, relishing *Weather:* taking it all in—its rich sensuality, its primal energy.

───❈───

Throughout its many retellings, the story of John Muir, storm-whipped at the top of the Douglas fir in the Yuba River valley, gradually took shape as a kind of icon of Christian spirituality for our family. The icon has been in place ever since as a standing rebuke against becoming a mere spectator to life, preferring creature comforts to Creator confrontations.

For spirituality has to do with life, *lived* life. For Christians, "spirituality" is derived (always and exclusively) from Spirit, God's Holy Spirit. And "spirit," in the biblical languages of Hebrew and Greek, is the word "wind," or "breeze," or "breath"—an invisibility that has visible effects.

This is the Wind/Spirit that created all the life we both see and can't see (Genesis 1:2); that created the life of Jesus (Luke 1:35 and 3:22); that created a church of worshiping men and women (Acts 2:2–4); that creates each Christian (Romans 8:11). There is no accounting for life, any life, except by means of this Wind/Spirit:

> Thou sendest forth thy spirit [breath/wind],
>> they are created:
> *and thou renewest the face of the earth.*
> *(Psalm 104:30 KJV)*

There is clearly far more to Spirit-created living than can be detected by blood pressure and pulse rate. All the "vital signs" of botany, biology, and physiology combined hardly begin to account for life; if it doesn't also extend into matters far more complex than our circulatory and respiratory systems—namely, matters of joy and love, faith and hope, truth and beauty, meaning and value—there is simply not enough there to qualify as "life" for the common run of human beings on this planet earth. Most of us may not be able to define "spirituality" in a satisfactory way, but few of us fail to recognize its presence or absence. And to feel ourselves enhanced by its presence and diminished by its absence. Life, life, and more life—it's our deepest hunger and thirst.

But that doesn't always translate into Spirit, Spirit, and more Spirit in the conduct of our lives. Spirit, *Holy* Spirit, in Christian terminology, is God's life in our lives, God living in us and thereby making us participants in the extravagant prodigality of life, visible and invisible, that is Spirit-created.

We humans, somewhere along the way, seem to have picked up the bad habit of trying to get life on our terms, without all the bother of God, the Spirit of Life. We keep trying to be our own gods; and we keep making a sorry mess of it. Worse, the word has gotten around in recent years that "spirituality" itself might be a way of getting a more intense life without having to deal with God—spirituality as a kind of intuitive bypass around the inconvenience of repentance and sacrifice and putting ourselves at risk by following Jesus in the way of the cross, the very way Jesus plainly told was the only way to the "abundant life" that he had come to bless us with.

The generic name for this way of going about things—trying to put together a life of meaning and security out of God-sanctioned stories and routines, salted with weekends of diversion and occasional erotic interludes, without dealing firsthand, believingly and obediently, with God—is "religion." It is not, of course, a life without God, but the God who is there tends to be mostly background and resource—a Quality or Being that provides the ideas and energy that I take charge of and arrange and use as I see fit. We all of us do it, more or less.

The word "religion," following one possible etymology (not all agree on this), comes from the Latin, *religere*, "to bind up, or tie up, again." The picture that comes to my mind is of myself, having spent years "getting it all together," strolling through John Muir's Yuba River valley, enjoying the country, whistling in self-satisfaction, carrying my "life" bundled in a neat package—memories and morals, goals and diversions, prayers and devotion all sorted and tied together. And then the storm comes, fierce and sudden, a gust tears my packaged life from my arms and scatters the items every which way, all over the valley, all through the forest.

What do I then do? Do I run helter-skelter through the trees, crawl through the brush, frantically trying to recover all the pieces of my life, desperately enlisting the help of passersby and calling in the experts, searching for and retrieving and putting back together again (rebinding!) whatever I can salvage of my life, and then hiding out in the warm and secure cabin until the storm blows over? Or do I follow John Muir to the exposed ridge and the top of the Douglas fir, and open myself to the Weather, not wanting to miss a detail of this invasion of Life into my life, ready at the drop of a hat to lose my life to save it (Mark 8:35)?

For me, the life of religion (cautious and anxious, holding things together as best I can so that my life will make sense and, hopefully, please God) and the life of spirituality (a passion for life and a willingness to risk identity and security in following Jesus, no matter what) contrast in these two scenarios. There is no question regarding what I want: I want to be out in the Weather! But far more often than not I find myself crawling around on the ground, gathering up the pieces of my life and tying them together again in a secure bundle, safe from the effects of the Weather. Actually, the two ways of life can coexist; there is, after all, a place for steady and responsible routine — John Muir, after all, didn't spend all his time at the top of the Douglas fir; he spent most of his time on the valley floor. He also had a cabin that he had built with his own hands in which he received guests and prepared meals for them. But if there is no readiness to respond to the living God, who moves when and how and where he chooses, it isn't much of a life — the *livingness* soon leaks out of it.

We cannot, of course, command Weather. It is there; it happens. There is no question of managing or directing it. There is no recipe for concocting "spirituality" any more than there is a chemical formula for creating "life." As Jesus most famously put it to that expert on the religious life, Nicodemus, "You know well enough how the wind blows this way and that. You hear it rustling through the trees, but you have no idea where it comes from or where it's headed next. That's the way it is with everyone 'born from above' by the wind of God, the Spirit of God" (John 3:8 THE MESSAGE).

The best we can do is to cultivate awareness, alertness, so that when the Wind blows we are *there*, ready to step into it—or not: when the absurd command comes to distribute the meager five loaves and two fish to the crowd we are ready to obey—or not; when direction is given to wait with the 120 for the promise, we are ready to wait—or not; when the invitation comes to "take ... eat ... drink," we are ready to come to the supper—or not.

<hr />

The books in this series, *Growing Deeper*, are what some of my friends and I do to stay alert and aware as we wait for the Wind to blow whether in furious storm or cooling breeze or gentle breathing—intending to cultivate and maintain a receptive readiness to the Spirit who brings us Life. They are not books *about* spirituality; they are simply accounts of what we do to stay awake to the Coming. There is nothing novel in any of them; our intent is to report what Christians have commonly done to stay present to the Spirit: we pray (Wangerin), preach and teach (Miller), meditate on the soul (Shaw), reflect on our checkered experiences with God's people (Yancey), and nurture Jesus-friends (Peterson).

Our shared conviction is that most of us in this "information age" have adequate access to facts; but in regards to *Life* (*Spirit*-formed spirituality), witness and motivation are always welcome.

Eugene H. Peterson
James Houston Professor of Spiritual Theology
Regent College
Vancouver, B.C., Canada

CHURCH:
WHY BOTHER?

CHAPTER 1

WHY BOTHER WITH CHURCH?

——— ◦◦◦◦ ———

This is a big old ship, Bill. She creaks, she rocks, she rolls, and at times she makes you want to throw up. But she gets where she's going. Always has, always will, until the end of time. With or without you.

J. F. POWERS, *WHEAT THAT SPRINGETH GREEN*

As I grew up in Georgia, church defined my life. I faithfully attended services every Sunday morning and evening and also on Wednesday nights, not to mention vacation Bible school, youth group activities, "revivals," missions conferences, and any other occasions when the doors might open. I looked at the world through stained-glass lenses: the church told me what to believe, who to trust or distrust, and how to behave.

During high school I attended church in a concrete-block building located on the grounds of a former pony farm. Several of the former stable buildings were still standing, littered with hay, and one Sunday morning the largest of these buildings burst into flames. Fire trucks noisily arrived, the deacons dashed about moving lumber and uncoiling hoses, and all of us church members stood and watched as orange flames climbed the sky and heat baked our faces. Then we solemnly filed back into the sanctuary, suffused with the scent of burnt straw and charred timbers, and listened to our pastor deliver an impromptu sermon on the fires of Hell which, he assured us, were seven times hotter than what we had just witnessed.

That image lived long in my mind because this was a "hellfire and brimstone" church. We saw ourselves as a huddled minority in a world fraught with danger. Any slight misstep might lead us away from safety toward the raging fires of Hell. Like the walls of a castle, church offered protection against that scary world outside.

My ventures into that outside world, especially in public high school, brought about some awkward moments. I remember the hot shame of standing before a high school speech class giving the pious reasons why I could not accompany them to view a Hollywood version of *Othello*. And even now I can quote the sarcastic words used by a biology teacher explaining to the class why my 20-page term paper had failed to demolish Charles Darwin's 592-page *Origin of Species*.

Yet I also recall the satisfying feeling that came from belonging to a persecuted minority. We congratulated ourselves for living "in the world" without being "of it." I felt like a spy, clutching some precious secret that few others knew about. "This world is not my home, I'm just a passin' through," we used to sing. During childhood and early adolescence, I rarely resented church: it was the lifeboat that carried me through the ocean swells of a turbulent world.

My church frowned on such activities as roller-skating (too much like dancing), bowling (some alleys serve liquor), going to movies, and reading the Sunday newspaper. The church erected this thick wall of external rules to protect us from the sinful world outside, and in a way it succeeded. Today I could do any of those activities with an unsullied conscience, yet I am also aware that the very strictness of fundamentalism kept me from deeper trouble. Strict legalism pulls in the boundaries of deviance: for example, we might sneak off to a bowling alley, but would never think of touching liquor or drugs.

Later, though, I came to view some of their rules as wholly arbitrary, and some as flat-out wrong. In the Deep South, racism was an integral part of the church subculture. I regularly heard from the pulpit that blacks—and that was not the word we used for them—were subhuman, ineducable, and cursed by God to be a "servant" race. Almost everyone in my church believed that Martin Luther King Jr. was "a card-carrying Communist"; we cheered every time a Southern sheriff hit him with a nightstick or locked him in jail.

A religion based on externals is easy to cast aside, and that is what I did for a period of time. When I moved out to taste the broader world for myself, I rejected the legalistic environment of my childhood. The words they used suddenly seemed deceptive, like Orwellian Newspeak. They talked about Grace but lived by Law; they spoke of love but showed signs of hate. Unfortunately, when I emerged from Southern fundamentalism, I cast off not just the shell of hypocrisy but also the body of belief.

Circling the Buttresses

I now see that the Deep South fundamentalism of my childhood represented far more than a place of worship or a spiritual community. It was a controlled environment, a subculture. I now recognize that a harsh church, full of fierce condemnation and empty of humility and any sense of mystery, stunted my faith for many years. In short, Christianity kept me from Christ. I have spent the rest of my life climbing back toward faith and climbing back toward church. My journey of return to faith is a long story that I dare not begin here. Rather, this small book centers on the blunt and simple question: Why bother with church?

Is church really necessary for a believing Christian? Winston Churchill once said that he related to the church rather like a flying buttress: he supported it from the outside. I tried that strategy for a while, after I had come to believe the doctrine sincerely and had committed myself to God. I am not alone. Far fewer people attend church on Sunday than claim to follow Christ. Some of them have stories similar to mine: they feel burned or even betrayed by a former church experience. Others simply "get nothing out of church." Following Jesus is one thing; following other Christians into a sanctuary on Sunday morning is quite another. Why bother? As the poet Anne Sexton put it,

> They pounded nails into his hands.
> After that, well, after that everyone wore hats ...

As I reflect on my pilgrimage, I can see that several barriers kept me away from church. First was hypocrisy. The atheistic philosopher Friedrich Nietzsche was once asked what made him so negative toward Christians. He replied, "I would believe in their salvation if they looked a little more like people who have been saved."

Scarred by the absolutist fundamentalism of my childhood, I too approached church warily. On Sunday mornings Christians dressed up in fine clothes and smiled at each other, but I knew from personal experience that such a façade could cloak a meaner spirit. I had a knee-jerk reaction against anything that smacked of hypocrisy until one day the question occurred to me, "What would church look like if every member were just like me?" Properly humbled, I began concentrating on my own spirituality, not everyone else's.

God is the ultimate judge of hypocrisy in the church, I decided; I would leave such judgment in God's capable hands. I began to relax and grow softer, more forgiving of others. After all, who has a perfect spouse, or perfect parents or children? We do not give up on the institution of family because of its imperfections—why give up on the church?

My next hurdle to overcome was cultural in nature. "Seeker churches" not yet having been invented, I discovered that the eleven o'clock hour on Sunday morning was oddly unlike any other hour in the week. At no other time did I sit for thirty or forty minutes in a straight-backed chair and listen to someone lecture me. At no other time did I sing songs written one or two centuries ago. I identified with one of Flannery O'Connor's in-laws, who started attending church because the service was "so horrible, he knew there must be something else there to make the people come."

O'Connor also said that she took care to be at her writing desk each morning so that, if an idea came, she would be there to receive it. A lapsed Catholic named Nancy Mairs writes in her memoirs *Ordinary Time* that she returned to church in somewhat the same way. Even while uncertain about belief in God, she began attending Mass again to prepare "a space into which belief could flood." She learned that one does not always go to church with belief in hand. Rather, one goes with open hands, and sometimes church fills them.

For me, the very structure of church got in the way of getting my hands filled. I enjoyed small groups where people talked about their lives, discussed matters of faith, and prayed together. A formal church service, though, with its unvarying routine, its repetitiveness, its crowds and bulletins and announcements, its conventions of standing up and sitting down, annoyed me. The longer you stay away from church the stranger it seems, and clearly I had got out of the habit.

It helped me to read accounts by C. S. Lewis and other notable Christians who wished to worship God but experienced church as a hindrance rather than a help. For instance, the Pulitzer Prize winner Annie Dillard once described her church this way,

> Week after week I was moved by the pitiableness of the bare linoleum-floored sacristy which no flowers could cheer or soften, by the terrible singing I so loved, by the fatigued Bible readings, the lagging emptiness and dilution of the liturgy, the horrifying vacuity of the sermon, and by the fog of dreary senselessness pervading the whole, which existed alongside, and probably caused, the wonder of the fact that we came; we returned; we showed up; week after week, we went through with it.

Even as I write these words, I must pause and shake my head in wonder. As I recollect my frame of mind from more than twenty years ago, it surprises me to recall how passionately I felt about such matters in my twenties. I have picked up the habit again, you see, and for years the church routine, this very routine that once so irked me, has seemed as comfortable as slipping on a pair of old shoes. I now like the hymns, I know when to stand and when to sit, I listen to the announcements because they involve activities I care about. Yet I force myself to remember what I felt back then because I know that for many people church still poses a cultural barrier difficult to overcome.

What changed my attitude toward church? A skeptic might say that I lowered my expectations somewhere along the way, or perhaps I "got used to" church just as, after numerous false starts, I got used to opera. Yet I sense something else at work: church has filled in me a need that could not be met in any other way. Saint John of the Cross wrote, "The virtuous soul that is alone ... is like the burning coal that is alone. It will grow colder rather than hotter." I believe he is right.

Christianity is not a purely intellectual, internal faith. It can only be lived in community. Perhaps for this reason, I have never entirely given up on church. At a deep level I sense that church contains something I desperately need. Whenever I abandon church for a time, I find that *I* am the one who suffers. My faith fades, and the crusty shell of lovelessness grows over me again. I grow colder rather than hotter. And so my journeys away from church have always circled back inside.

Nowadays, despite my checkered churchgoing past, I could hardly imagine life without church. When my wife and I moved to another state, finding a church was one of our most urgent priorities. If we missed a Sunday, we felt a void.

How did I move from being a skeptic of the church to an advocate, from a spectator to a participant? Can I identify what rehabilitated my attitude toward church? I would respond by saying that over the years I have learned what to look for in a church. In childhood I had no more choice over church than I had over what school I attended. Later, I exercised much choice over church, trying first this one and then that one. The process taught me that the key to finding the right church lay inside me. It involved *my way of seeing*. Once I learned how to look, issues such as what denomination a church belonged to mattered far less.

When I go to church, I have learned to look up, look around, look outward, and look inward. This new way of seeing has helped me to stop merely tolerating the church and instead learn to love it.

I present these observations in full knowledge that some people—those who live in small towns, for instance—have few options of churches to attend. Yet I believe that for all of us, a way of seeing can transform our understanding of what church was meant to be. Once we have a vision of the church, as participants we can help it become the kind of place God intended.

Looking Up

I used to approach church with the spirit of a discriminating consumer. I viewed the worship service as a performance. Give me something I like. Entertain me.

Speaking of folks like me, Søren Kierkegaard said that we tend to think of church as a kind of theater: we sit in the audience, attentively watching the actor on-stage, who draws every eye to himself. If sufficiently entertained, we show our gratitude with applause and cheers. Church, though, should be the opposite of the theater. In church *God* is the audience for our worship. Far from playing the role of the leading actor, the minister should function as something like a prompter, the inconspicuous helper who sits beside the stage and prompts by whispering.

What matters most takes place within the hearts of the congregation, not among the actors onstage. We should leave a worship service asking ourselves not "What did I get out of it?" but rather "Was God pleased with what happened?" Now I try to look up in a worship service, to direct my gaze beyond the platform, toward God.

Such a change in viewpoint has helped me to cope with the talent deficit I encounter in various churches. To direct the spotlight away from the minister, some churches seek to involve many lay people in worship. They compose songs or poetry, act out mini-dramas, sing in trios, make banners, express themselves through sacred dance. I confess that, judged by objective standards of esthetics and even by the subjective standards of "worship promptings," many of these attempts do little to enhance my own worship. Gradually, though, the truth has sunk in that God, not the congregation, is the audience who matters most.

I am trying to learn a lesson from C. S. Lewis, who wrote this about his church:

> I disliked very much their hymns, which I considered to be fifth-rate poems set to sixth-rate music. But as I went on I saw the great merit of it.... I realized that the hymns (which were just sixth-rate music) were, nevertheless, being sung with devotion and benefit by an old saint in elastic-side boots in the opposite pew, and then you realize that you aren't fit to clean those boots. It gets you out of your solitary conceit.

Church exists primarily not to provide entertainment or to encourage vulnerability or to build self-esteem or to facilitate friendships but to worship God; if it fails in that, it fails. I have learned that the ministers, the music, the sacraments, and the other "trappings" of worship are mere promptings to support the ultimate goal of getting worshipers in touch with God. If ever I doubt this fact, I go back and read the Old Testament, which devotes nearly as much space to specifications for worship in the tabernacle and the temple as the New Testament devotes to the life of Christ. Taken as a whole, the Bible clearly puts the emphasis on what pleases God—the point of worship, after all. To worship, says Walter Wink, is to remember Who owns the house.

In church I can look toward the platform, as a spectator, or I can look up, toward God. The same God who took pains to specify details of animal sacrifice for the ancient Israelites later told them, "I have no need of a bull from your stall or of goats from your pen, for every animal of the forest is mine, and the cattle on a thousand hills." By focusing on the externals of worship, they had missed the point entirely: he was interested in a sacrifice of the heart, an internal attitude of submission and thanksgiving. Now, when I attend church, I try to focus on that internal spirit rather than sitting back in my pew, like a theater critic, making esthetic judgments.

I have visited Roman Catholic and Russian Orthodox worship services that utterly defy the consumer mentality prevalent in America. Most Catholic services de-emphasize the sermon, or "homily," and few priests I have heard would score well in a preaching contest. When I ask about this weakness, they shrug it off. For them the sacrament of communion, or Mass, is the center of worship; they serve as prompters.

In Russian Orthodox churches, priests do not even speak the language of the people, since few congregants can understand the Old Slavonic specified for worship. Choirs chant out the message of the gospel, and many services dispense with the sermon altogether. What matters is worship: again, the priest, the icons, the church architecture, the incense, and the choir serve as prompters.

For many reasons I continue to worship in the Protestant tradition, which places a greater emphasis on the Word spoken from the pulpit. Yet I no longer worry so much about the style of music, the order of worship, the "trappings" of church, as I once did in my days of church-shopping. By focusing on the trappings and not the goal of worship—to meet God—I had missed the most important message of all.

Looking Around

Early in my pilgrimage back toward church, I made the mistake of intentionally seeking out churches composed of people like me. I was looking for a congregation of my educational level, with my biblical background and my taste in hymns and liturgy. In an odd way, I was repeating the mistake of my childhood church, which tried to stamp out any sign of diversity. That church admitted no people of color, mocked the emotional style of worship in black churches across town, and railed against Pentecostals and others who had a different view of spiritual gifts. As a result we had an impoverished, starched-shirt form of worship.

In the 1960s Martin Luther King Jr. used to say (quoting Billy Graham) that 11:00 A.M. on Sunday was the most segregated hour in America, and now Jesse Jackson can safely repeat the same saying. Little has changed to bring heterogeneity to worship—indeed, church growth experts caution against it. Government and industry have experimented with affirmative action plans and quota systems in an attempt to redress injustices from the past, yet have never heard of a church launching an affirmative action plan in order to increase participation from minorities.

Although I have attended numerous churches in the past few decades, much of what I have learned about church traces back to LaSalle Street Church in downtown Chicago. LaSalle had the same clash over worship styles, the same struggle with finances, the same mixture of committed and uncommitted Christians that can be found in most churches. By no means was it a perfect church. Yet as I now look back on the thirteen years I spent there, I see that in several important ways it taught me what the church could be and should be.

When I began attending LaSalle Street Church, I had resigned myself to church as a necessary spiritual discipline. To my surprise, Sunday morning soon became something that I looked forward to rather than dreaded. Why? I credit the delightful mix of people who attended LaSalle. There, I learned to look around me as well as up. I worshiped among people who were decidedly not like me.

The church stood midway between the richest and poorest communities of Chicago. Two blocks to the east lay the Gold Coast, average income over $50,000; two blocks to the west lay the Cabrini-Green housing project, average income under $3,500. LaSalle sought the role of a "bridge church" between the two neighborhoods. A man named Bill Leslie served as pastor, and Bill and I shared a common background in racist fundamentalism. He had been student body president at the strictly segregated Bob Jones University, and his father-in-law had worked in segregationist Lester Maddox's gubernatorial campaign in Georgia. Perhaps in reaction, Bill made racial reconciliation a primary goal of the church.

LaSalle was the first church to give me a taste of wide diversity. On Sunday mornings volunteers cooked a free breakfast—the smell of biscuits and ham does a lot for a sanctuary, I found — for senior citizens, many of whom stayed for worship. Half the seniors were African-American, half were white. On cold mornings homeless street people would wander in for breakfast too, and sometimes these visitors would stretch out on the pews and snore loudly through the morning service.

The congregation also included graduate students enrolled in Ph.D. programs at prestigious schools like Northwestern and the University of Chicago, as well as doctors, lawyers, and other well-educated professionals. Because of this mixture, whenever I taught classes or occasionally preached I was forced to keep the gospel to a common level. Did my words hold meaning for a bag lady as well as for a theological student?

I came to marvel at the gospel's ability to speak simultaneously to rich professionals and also street people with no education. And I began to look forward to church as a place that surrounded me with people different from me. On the surface we had little in common; our commitment to Jesus Christ, however, gave us much in common.

I once attended a weekend retreat led by Scott Peck, who had invited together ten Jews, ten Christians, and ten Muslims in order to test out his theory of community. Peck believes that most people have it backwards: we think that community comes after diverse people resolve their conflicts. In the Middle East, for example, leaders of hostile states get together and hammer out peace agreements, and after that people may (or may not) learn to live in peace. According to Peck, peace might come more naturally if the leaders learn to live in community *first*, and then work on resolving their conflicts.

I will always be grateful for that weekend with Scott Peck because it taught me what community within the church could, and should, strive toward. The Christian basis for community, the reconciling love of God, transcends all differences of nationality, race, class, age, and gender. Our commonality comes first; the issues that divide us come later.

At LaSalle Street Church, and a few other places, I have seen glimpses of what can happen when community forms around what we hold in common. A family of God emerges, one in which unity does not mean uniformity and diversity does not mean division.

How easily we forget that the Christian church was the first institution in the history of the world to bring together on equal footing Jews and Gentiles, men and women, slaves and free.

The earliest Christians broke down barriers. Unlike most other religions, Christians welcomed men and women alike. The Greeks excluded slaves from most social groupings, while Christians included them. The Jewish temple separated worshipers by race and gender; Christians brought them together around the Lord's table. In contrast to Rome's mostly male aristocracy, the Christian church let women and the poor take leadership roles.

The Apostle Paul, a "Hebrew of the Hebrews," waxed eloquent on this "mystery, which for ages past was kept hidden in God." God's intent, said Paul, "was that now, through the church, the manifold wisdom of God should be made known to the rulers and authorities in the heavenly realms" (Ephesians 3:9–10). By forming a community out of diverse members, we have the opportunity to capture the attention of the world and even the supernatural world beyond.

I realize, of course, that diversity comes in different forms. Even all-white or all-black churches have a diversity in age groups and educational background and economic class. Church is the one place I go in a week that brings together generations: infants still held at their mothers' breasts, children who squirm and giggle at all the wrong times, responsible adults who know how to act appropriately at all times, and senior citizens who are liable to drift off asleep if the preacher drones on too long.

Now, when I look for a church, I look around me at the people sitting in the pews or chairs. I have much to learn from the uninhibited worship styles of African-Americans and Pentecostals, from the stalwart faith of senior citizens, from the daily struggles of moms with preschool children. I deliberately seek a congregation composed of people *not* like me.

Looking Outward

The church, said Archbishop William Temple, is "the only cooperative society in the world that exists for the benefit of its non-members." That is the lesson I learned most clearly from LaSalle Street Church. The churches of my childhood had always emphasized foreign missions, and I looked forward to the annual missions conference with its displays of blowguns and spears and tribal masks. In Chicago, though, I learned that the mission of the church extends to the needs of its own neighborhood. One of the reasons the congregation of such diversity worked well was that we banded together to reach out to the community around us. Actively serving others causes you to think less about serving yourself.

Neighborhood programs at LaSalle began when Sunday school teachers, noticing that many students could not read, offered tutoring classes after the Sunday service. The need was enormous, since the local high school's dropout rate exceeded seventy-five percent. Soon busloads of students from Wheaton College were making their way to LaSalle Street to help with one-on-one teaching. IBM and other companies donated equipment, and a state-of-the-art tutoring program grew out of these early efforts.

To counter neighborhood abuse by the police and by landlords, an attorney quit his firm to begin a Legal Aid Clinic, offering free legal representation to any housing project resident with qualifying income. A counseling center was established, with sliding fees based on income. In Chicago, as in most U.S. cities, the majority of babies are born to single mothers, and soon the church founded a ministry to assist them as well.

More needs surfaced. When a government study reported that a third of all dog and cat food was purchased by senior citizens too poor to afford "people food," the church began a ministry to local seniors. The director organized bingo games, a favorite among the seniors, featuring not money but canned goods as prizes; the seniors had fun, won bags of food, and left with their dignity intact.

For eleven years my wife Janet directed the church's senior citizens program. She relied on seventy volunteers, and I learned through her how much good can be accomplished by a congregation of ordinary people who band together to minister to the needs around them. A local radio disc jockey in a red sports car would pull up to a dilapidated house each week and deliver groceries to a homebound senior. A young lawyer would take his children on weekly visits to a blind man in a nursing home. A nurse from the church made house calls. Twice a week volunteers cooked meals—for many seniors, the only hot meals they would eat all week. Many of these people volunteered out of a sense of guilt or responsibility. Over time, however, they learned that one of the main benefits of giving is its effect on the giver. Our need to give is every bit as desperate as the poor's need to receive.

Evangelist Luis Palau captured the nature of the church in an earthy metaphor. The church, he said, is like manure. Pile it together and it stinks up the neighborhood; spread it out and it enriches the world. When I look for a church, I look for one that understands the need to look outward. Indeed, I have come to believe that outreach may be the most important factor in a church's success or failure.

Suburban churches may have to look harder for outreach opportunities; they may involve a tie-in with the inner city, or a connection with a program in Russia or a sister church in Latin America. Such outreach may at first seem like a drain of energy and resources. I have found it to be just the opposite. In a paradox of faith, the one who shares love comes away enriched, not impoverished.

Looking Inward

Perhaps in reaction against the legalism of his childhood, Bill Leslie, the pastor at LaSalle Street Church, never tired of the theme of Grace: he recognized his own endless need for grace, preached it almost every Sunday, and offered it to everyone around him in starkly practical ways. As I sat under his ministry Sunday after Sunday I gradually absorbed grace, as if by osmosis. I came to believe, truly believe, that God loves me not because I deserve it but because he is a God of grace. God's love comes free of charge, with no strings attached. There is nothing I can do to make God love me more—or less.

Grace, I concluded, was the factor most glaringly absent from my childhood church. If only our churches could communicate grace to a world of competition, judgment, and ranking—a world of ungrace—then church would become a place where people gather eagerly, without coercion, like desert nomads around an oasis. Now, when I attend church, I look inward and ask God to purge from me the poisons of rivalry and criticism and to fill me with grace. And I seek out churches characterized by a state of grace.

I learned an enduring lesson about what grace looks like in action from my church's response to Adolphus, a young black man with a wild, angry look in his eye. Every inner-city church has at least one Adolphus. He had spent some time in Vietnam, and most likely his troubles started there. He could never hold a job for long. His fits of rage and craziness sometimes landed him in an asylum.

If Adolphus took his medication on Sunday, he was manageable. Otherwise, well, church could be even more exciting than usual. He might start at the back and high-hurdle his way over the pews down to the altar. He might raise his hands in the air during a hymn and make obscene gestures. Or he might wear headphones and tune in rap music instead of the sermon.

As part of worship, LaSalle had a time called "Prayers of the People." We would all stand, and spontaneously various people would call out a prayer—for peace in the world, for healing of the sick, for justice in the community around us. "Lord, hear our prayer," we would respond in unison after each spoken request. Adolphus soon figured out that Prayers of the People provided an ideal platform for him to air his concerns.

"Lord, thank you for creating Whitney Houston and her magnificent body!" he prayed one morning. After a puzzled pause, a few chimed in weakly, "Lord, hear our prayer."

"Lord, thank you for the big recording contract I signed last week, and for all the good things happening to my band!" prayed Adolphus. Those of us who knew Adolphus realized he was fantasizing, but others joined in with a heartfelt "Lord, hear our prayer."

Regular attenders came to expect the unexpected from Adolphus's prayers. Visitors had no idea what to think: their eyes would snap open and their necks would crane to get a look at the source of these unusual prayers.

Adolphus called down judgment on all the white people in the church who had caused Mayor Harold Washington such stress that he had a heart attack. He railed against President George Bush who sent troops against Iraq while people were being killed in the streets of Chicago. He gave regular reports on the progress of his music group. Some of these prayers were met with an awkward silence. Once Adolphus prayed "that the white honkey pastors of this church would see their houses burn down this week." No one seconded that prayer.

Adolphus had already been kicked out of three other churches. He preferred attending an integrated church because he enjoyed making white people squirm. Once he stood up in a Sunday school class I was teaching and said, "If I had an M-16 rifle I would kill all you people in this room." We white people squirmed.

A group of people in the church, including a doctor and a psychiatrist, took on Adolphus as a special project. Every time he had an outburst, they pulled him aside and talked it through, using the word "inappropriate" a lot. "Adolphus, your anger may be justified. But there are appropriate and inappropriate ways to express it. Praying for the pastor's house to burn down is inappropriate."

We learned that Adolphus sometimes walked the five miles to church on Sunday because he could not afford the bus fare. Members of the congregation began to offer him rides. Some invited him over for meals. Most Christmases, he spent with our assistant pastor's family.

Boasting about his musical talent, Adolphus asked to join the music group that sang during communion services. It turned out that he had absolutely no musical ability. After hearing him audition, the leader settled on a compromise: Adolphus could stand with the others and sing, but only if his electric guitar remained unplugged. Each time the group performed thereafter, Adolphus stood with them and sang and played his guitar, which, thankfully, produced no sound. Generally this compromise worked well, except for the Sundays when Adolphus skipped his medication and felt led to do a gyrating Joe Cocker imitation across the platform as the rest of us lined up to receive the body and blood of Christ.

The day came when Adolphus asked to join the church. Elders quizzed him on his beliefs, found little by way of encouragement, and decided to put him on a kind of probation. He could join when he demonstrated that he understood what it meant to be a Christian, they decided, and when he learned to act appropriately around others in church.

Against all odds, Adolphus's story has a happy ending. He calmed down. He started calling people in the church when he felt the craziness coming on. He even got married. And on the third try Adolphus was finally accepted for church membership.

Grace comes to people who do not deserve it, and for me Adolphus came to represent grace. In his entire life, no one had ever invested that kind of energy and concern in him. He had no family, he had no job, he had no stability. Church became for him the one stable place. It accepted him despite all he had done to earn rejection.

The church did not give up on Adolphus. It gave him a second chance, and a third, and a fourth. Christians who had experienced God's grace transferred it to Adolphus, and that stubborn, unquenchable grace gave me an indelible picture of what God puts up with by choosing to love the likes of me. I now look for churches that exude this kind of grace.

A New Sign on the Beach

"There are two things we cannot do alone," said Paul Tournier: "one is to be married and the other is be a Christian." In my pilgrimage with the church, I have learned that the church plays a vital, even necessary role. We are God's "new community" on earth.

I am aware, painfully aware, that the kind of church I have described, the ideal church I look for, is the exception, not the norm. Many churches offer more entertainment than worship, more uniformity than diversity, more exclusivity than outreach, more law than grace. Nothing troubles my faith more than my disappointment with the visible church.

Still, I must remind myself of Jesus' words to his disciples, "You did not choose me, but I chose you." The church was God's risk, his "gamble," so to speak. I have even come to see in the church's flawed humanity a paradoxical sign of hope. God has paid the human race the ultimate compliment, by choosing to live within us vessels of clay.

Several times I have read the Bible straight through, from Genesis to Revelation, and each time it strikes me that the church is a culmination, the realization of what God had in mind from the beginning. The Body of Christ becomes an overarching new identity that breaks down barriers of race and nationality and gender and makes possible a community that exists nowhere else in the world. Simply read the first paragraph from each of Paul's letters to diverse congregations scattered throughout the Roman Empire. They are all "in Christ," and that matters even more than their race or economic status or any of the other categories humanity may devise.

My identity in Christ is more important than my identity as an American or as a Coloradan or as a white male or as a Protestant. Church is the place where I celebrate that new identity and work it out in the midst of people who have many differences but share this one thing in common. We are charged to live out a kind of alternative society before the eyes of the watching world, a world that is increasingly moving toward tribalism and division.

One scene from my time at LaSalle Street Church stands in my memory as a vivid picture of this new community. Each year in the summer, LaSalle held a baptism service in always-frigid Lake Michigan. I remember one year especially, a gloriously sunny day when Chicago's ethnic life was splayed out for all to see. The melting pot simmered: dudes on roller skates decked out in plastic helmets and kneepads, cyclists honking for sidewalk space, buttered bodies stretched out in a random pattern on the beach.

In the midst of this beachfront scene, thirteen baptismal candidates lined up to speak. There were two young stockbrokers, husband and wife, who said they wanted to "identify with Christ more publicly." A woman of Cuban descent spoke, dressed all in white. A tall, bronzed man said he had been an agnostic until six months ago. An aspiring opera singer admitted she had just decided to seek baptism that morning and asked for prayer because she hates cold water. An eighty-five-year-old black woman had asked to be immersed against her doctor's advice ("Strangest request I ever heard," he said). A real estate investor, a pregnant woman, a medical student, and a few others each took turns explaining why they too had come to seek immersion off North Avenue Beach.

The bodies were dipped rather quickly. Each baptismal candidate emerged from the water trembling and goosepimply, eyes bright and large from the cold. Those of us on shore greeted them with hugs, and as a result wet spots soon appeared on our chests. "Welcome to the Body of Christ," we said.

During these proceedings, I kept glancing around at the Chicago bystanders. A few disgruntled sun worshipers moved away muttering. Most were tolerant, though, responding with stares and bemused smiles. Just another weird religious group, they probably thought.

After an hour, the church group departed. The scene at North Avenue Beach soon filled in the space our little band had occupied by the water's edge. Our footprints were washed away, our sand redoubt was quickly covered with towels and sunbathers.

That small scene at the beach, worked out before a curious crowd, became for me a symbol of the alternative society that Jesus inaugurated on earth so long ago. Chicago's beaches have their own pecking order: Hispanics to the north, yuppies near the lifeguard tower, gays by the rocks. Like gathers with like, families stick together. This small community, though, encompassed stockbrokers and Cubans, an opera singer, and an eighty-five-year-old granddaughter of slaves.

Moreover, we had assembled to declare our allegiance to another kingdom altogether, a kingdom that for us takes priority over the sensual pleasures afforded by a lazy Sunday at the beach. As each baptismal candidate was presented, someone from the church prayed aloud for that person's new walk with God. One, in his prayer, quoted Jesus' promise that great rejoicing breaks out in heaven when a sinner repents.

Seen from the lifeguard tower at North Avenue Beach, not much happened that Sunday afternoon. Seen from another viewpoint, that of eternity, a celebration sprang to life that will never end.

My favorite definition of the church comes from Karl Barth, who said, "[The Church] exists ... to set up in the world a new sign which is radically dissimilar to [the world's] own manner and which contradicts it in a way which is full of promise." Our ceremony along the shoreline of Lake Michigan was indeed radically dissimilar to the world's — or at least Chicago's — own manner. And my experience with the church, LaSalle Street Church in particular, had proven to me that the church can contradict the world in a way which is full of promise.

That very morning volunteers at the church had cooked a breakfast of eggs, ham, and biscuits for any hungry person who walked through the door — this in an era of reduced welfare and government entitlements. While politicians were voting funds for new jails and promising a crackdown on crime, LaSalle lawyers were counseling young criminals and tutors were teaching them to read. While sociologists were debating new ways to stigmatize mothers who bore children out of wedlock, a church program was helping those same women cope with the practical consequences of a difficult choice against abortion. While developers were demolishing single room occupancy hotels and replacing them with luxury condos, church elders were drawing up plans for senior citizens' housing. We did those things in large part because of what took place that morning in Lake Michigan: because we were joined together in a new identity in Christ Jesus, who broke down the walls of partition.

Having experienced the grace of God for ourselves, we wanted to dispense it to others, free of charge, no strings attached, as grace always comes. The church, I have learned, can indeed be a new sign radically dissimilar to the world's own manner, and contradict it in a way which is full of promise. For this reason, church is worth the bother.

CHAPTER 2

WHAT GOD HAD IN MIND

———— ✺ ————

To dwell in love with saints above,
Why that will be glory.
To dwell below with saints I know —
Why, that's a different story.

ANONYMOUS

t did not take long for me to notice that LaSalle Street Church was no ordinary church. On my very first visit I found a seat directly behind a middle-aged black woman and her thirteen-year-old daughter. When we stood to sing, the girl turned around and grinned at those of us in the pew behind her. We smiled back politely, and she continued grinning and staring at us. She seemed a little strange, perhaps even retarded. During the fourth stanza of the hymn she bent over, grabbed the hem of her skirt, and lifted it over her head, exposing herself. Welcome to church.

Over the next few years, we learned to count on the unexpected. One Sunday a man aimed a football, a perfect spiral pass, at the pastor who stood at the altar praying over a full tray of communion glasses. (He opened his eyes just in time to dodge the missile.) Another Sunday a homeless man drank an entire tray of thimble-size glasses, evidently unaware that we used grape juice for communion and not wine. Once a street woman wrapped in many skirts wandered to the platform during the sermon, genuflected, and started talking aloud to the visiting speaker about the poison found in milk cartons.

I remember sitting next to a visitor one Sunday, a woman of about fifty, beautifully dressed in a silk blouse and crushed-velvet skirt. She wore diamond earrings, and her streaked hair was pulled back dramatically from her forehead. I had no clue that she might be slightly unbalanced until she burst out laughing when a senior citizen accidentally lit the wrong advent candle. (The senior must have heard the laugh. "So sorry," she stammered. "I saw the pretty pink candle and my eyes went right to it, just like a little kid.") The visitor then leaned over to ask me about the half-burned purple candle, and I tried in vain to explain the advent candle tradition. "That's ridiculous!" she said. "They ought to throw that used candle away."

The visitor then proceeded to give a running commentary during the entire service. She laughed out loud when the pastor broke the communion bread: "Doesn't he know about the new wafers?" She made fun of people going forward to receive communion: "Those people are like zombies up there—why don't they loosen up?" When a doctor made an announcement about forming a new AIDS task force, she whispered, "That's disgusting—talking about AIDS in church!" And when the pastor in his sermon mentioned the word *Yahweh*, she nearly bolted. "That word is so primitive!" she said. "Does he realize how old-fashioned he is?"

After the service finally ended, the visitor slipped on a mink coat, introduced herself to me as "Vicki," and said, "That's the most unusual Mass I've ever been to. The people in this place crack me up. Why wasn't everyone laughing?"

I tried to explain a few things about our church, but it occurred to me later that, really, Vicki had asked a very good question.

Groping for Words

A downtown church that does not turn away the poor, the homeless, or the unpredictable, risks attracting people who may disrupt the worship service. In my years at LaSalle Street Church I learned that God is surely as present in the midst of such barely controlled chaos as in the well-orchestrated suburban churches I had come from. The church, as Eugene Peterson has observed, is composed of equal parts mystery and mess.

I think of urban churches like LaSalle whenever I read Paul's letters to the church in Corinth. There, too, a spirit of barely controlled chaos reigned. The letters spell out the makeup of the congregation: Jewish merchants, gypsies, Greeks, prostitutes, pagan idolaters. No other New Testament books reveal such violent swings in tone. Paul battled church schisms, harangued them about a case of incest, and fought to keep the Lord's Supper from turning into a free-for-all. Corinth makes my church seem boring.

Most scholars believe that 1 Corinthians predates virtually every other book in the New Testament. The first few chapters show the apostle struggling with a basic question: "Just what is this thing called a 'church'?" Paul had never asked such questions about Judaism: culture, religious tradition, race, and even the physical character-istics of worshipers clearly established the identity of that religion. But what was a Christian church? What did God have in mind? The answer must have seemed elusive indeed in the unruly context of Corinth. Almost twenty centuries later, the answer still seems elusive to me.

Paul's letter to Corinth betrays his hesitation, mainly in the way he gropes for words. You are God's field, he says in chapter 3, and explores that metaphor for a while: I, Paul, resemble a farmer who plants while another person waters. On the other hand, you are more like God's building. Yes, exactly. I lay the foundation, and someone else adds the next layer. Better yet, you're a temple, a building designed to house God. Yes, indeed! Think about that: God living in you, his sacred building.

Field, building, temple — make up your mind, Paul, I think to myself as I read through the succession of metaphors. He continues in such a vein throughout the book until finally, in chapter 12, he seizes upon a metaphor that fits best: the church as God's body. The book changes tone at that point, its style elevating from that of personal correspondence to the magnificent prose of chapter 13.

I believe that we have, in 1 Corinthians, a record of Paul thinking out loud, trying out ways of describing this thing called church. Each new metaphor casts a different light on the subject, and the last one, the body, seems the most accurate description of all. Paul spends an entire chapter exploring physiological parallels, and his letters return to that same metaphor of body more than two dozen times.

As a writer, I identify closely with Paul's style conveyed in these chapters. I often go through a similar procedure of searching for precisely the right word or metaphor: experimenting with this one, discarding that one, trying to force one, and then, *ahh*, experiencing the fine sense of relief that comes with locating the word or phrase that truly fits.

And yet, because of the years that have elapsed, not all of Paul's images of the church communicate so well today. Although the truth they point to has not changed, the perspective of the readers has greatly changed. Consider the illustrations from farming. Every Corinthian knew what they meant, for farms and vineyards surrounded their city and they bought their produce from farmers at a local bazaar. Nowadays, from modern cities in the U.S. you must travel at least thirty miles to see a respectable farm, and food comes scrubbed and shrink-wrapped on the shelves of a grocery store. For urbanites, the metaphor has lost its immediacy.

The building metaphor has a similar problem. In first-century Corinth you could buy a load of blocks and lay out a foundation, a process requiring no more skill than the ability to dig a ditch and follow a straight line. Now you need building permits, jackhammers, backhoes, forms assemblers, re-bars, concrete contractors (with union cards, please), and a general contractor to supervise it all. Somewhere in all the specialization, the force of the metaphor dissipates. As for Paul's reference to temples, who builds temples anymore?

What would Paul, the master of metaphor, say if he wrote 1 Corinthians today—if he was writing, say, to the First Presbyterian Church in Spokane, Washington, or to St. Mark's Episcopal Church in Atlanta, Georgia, or LaSalle Street Church in downtown Chicago? What word pictures would best communicate to us moderns what God had in mind for the church?

I cannot guess what Paul might have written, but I have let my mind roam over what exists in the world around me, searching for images that might apply to the church. I have asked myself, What is this thing called church? What is it supposed to be?

I have attended many churches, and none match my ideal. Even so, I can see value in spending some time thinking about the ideal. Olympic athletes use the technique of mentally visualizing each stage of the race or the routine just before stepping up to compete. When I first learned to downhill ski, a friend loaned me a "cybernetics" video on skiing, based on the theory that you can prepare your brain in advance before venturing out on a slope. The video showed skiers up-weighting, carving turns, and shifting body positions as they moved down the mountain. I worked hard to master the theory of skiing before putting it into practice on the mountain. In no way did I look like the video athletes when I stepped on the mountain. I fell, I made turns with jerky motions, I overreacted and shifted my weight at all the wrong times. Yet it helped to have the ideal imprinted in my brain as I fumbled my way down the mountain. At least I knew what I was doing wrong.

The images that Paul used may have served a similar function for Corinth. To a bunch of uncoordinated snowplowers, Paul was painting a picture of elegant slaloming. What follows are my own updated pictures of the church, drawn from all the churches I have attended. Every church shoots for an ideal, and every church misses the mark. But at least a picture of the ideal gives us something to shoot for.

God's Twelve-Step Group

I once visited a "church" that manages, with no denominational headquarters or paid staff, to attract millions of devoted members each week. It goes by the name Alcoholics Anonymous. I went at the invitation of a friend who had just confessed to me his problem with drinking. "Come along," he said, "and I think you'll catch a glimpse of what the early church must have been like."

At twelve o'clock on a Monday night I entered a ramshackle house that had been used for six other sessions already that day. Acrid clouds of cigarette smoke hung like tear gas in the air, stinging my eyes. It did not take long, however, to understand what my friend had meant with his comparison to the early church.

A well-known politician and several prominent millionaires were mixing freely with unemployed dropouts and kids with needle marks on their arms. Introductions went like this: "Hi, I'm Tom, and I'm an alcoholic and a drug addict." Instantly everyone shouted out warmly, "Hi, Tom!"

The "sharing time" worked like the textbook description of a small group, marked by compassionate listening, warm responses, and many hugs. Each person attending gave a personal progress report on his or her battle with addiction. We laughed a lot, and we cried a lot. Mostly, the members seemed to enjoy being around people who could see right through their façades. There was no reason not to be honest; everyone was in the same boat.

AA owns no property, has no headquarters, no media center, no staff of well-paid consultants and investment counselors who jet across the country. The original founders of AA built in safeguards that would kill off anything that might lead to a bureaucracy, believing their program could work only if it stayed at the most basic, intimate level: one alcoholic devoting his or her life to help another. Yet AA has proven so effective that 250 other kinds of twelve-step groups, from Chocoholics Anonymous to cancer patient groups, have sprung up in conscious mimicry of its technique.

The many parallels to the early church are no mere historical accidents. The Christian founders of AA insisted that dependence on God be a mandatory part of the program. The night I attended, everyone in the room repeated aloud the twelve steps, which acknowledge total dependence on God for forgiveness and strength. (Agnostic members may substitute the euphemism "Higher Power," but after a while that begins to seem inane and impersonal and they usually revert to "God.")

My friend freely admits that AA has replaced the church for him, and this fact sometimes troubles him. "AA groups borrow the sociology of the church, along with a few of the words and concepts, but they have no underlying doctrine," he says. "I miss that, but mainly I'm trying to survive, and AA helps me in that struggle far better than any local church." Others in the group explain their ecclesiastical resistance by recounting stories of rejection and judgment. A local church is the last place they would stand up and declare, "Hi, I'm Tom. I'm an alcoholic and a drug addict."

For my friend, immersion into Alcoholics Anonymous has meant salvation in the most literal sense. He knows that one slip could—no, will—send him to an early grave. More than once his AA partner has responded to his calls at 4:00 A.M., only to find him slouched in the eerie brightness of an all-night restaurant where he is filling a notebook, like a punished schoolchild, with the single sentence, "God help me make it through the next five minutes."

I came away from the "midnight church" impressed, yet also troubled that AA meets needs in a way that the local church does not—or at least did not, for my friend. I asked him to name the one quality missing in the local church that AA had somehow provided. He stared at his cup of coffee for a long time, watching it go cold. I expected to hear a word like love or acceptance or, knowing him, perhaps anti-institutionalism. Instead, he said softly this one word: dependency.

"None of us can make it on our own—isn't that why Jesus came?" he explained. "Yet most church people give off a self-satisfied air of piety or superiority. I don't sense them consciously leaning on God or on each other. Their lives appear to be in order. An alcoholic who goes to church feels inferior and incomplete." He sat in silence for a while, until a smile began to crease his face. "It's a funny thing," he said at last. "What I hate most about myself, my alcoholism, was the one thing God used to bring me back to him. Because of it, I know I can't survive without God. I have to depend on him to make it through each and every day. Maybe that's the redeeming value of alcoholism. Maybe God is calling us alcoholics to teach the saints what it means to be dependent on him and on his community on earth."

From my friend's midnight church I learned the need for humility, total honesty, and radical dependence—on God and on a community of compassionate friends. As I thought about it, these qualities seemed exactly what Jesus had in mind when he founded his church.

According to historian Ernest Kurtz, Alcoholics Anonymous came out of a discovery Bill Wilson made in his first meeting with Doctor Bob Smith. On his own, Bill had stayed sober for six months until he made a trip out of town, where a business deal fell through. Depressed, wandering a hotel lobby, he heard familiar sounds of laughter and of ice tinkling in glasses. He headed toward the bar, thinking "I need a drink."

Suddenly a brand new thought came to him, stopping him in his tracks: "No, I don't need a drink—I need another alcoholic!" Walking instead toward the lobby telephones, he began the sequence of calls that put him in touch with Dr. Smith, who would become AA's cofounder.

Church is a place where I can say, unashamedly, "I don't need to sin. I need another sinner." Perhaps together we can keep each other accountable, on the path.

God's Driver's License Bureau

Quite frankly, much of my time I spend around people very much like me. For the most part my friends resemble me in education, age, and values; they drive similar cars and have similar tastes in coffee, books, and music. I know about various ethnic groups—a million Poles in Chicago, for example, and many Hispanics where I now live, in Colorado—but I rarely run into them. (I tried shopping in a Hispanic grocery store, but got hopelessly lost in the two long aisles devoted to different varieties of beans.)

Every three years, however, I get a notice ordering me to report to the Driver's License Bureau to renew my license. Sometimes I have to take a written test, sometimes merely fill out a form and pose for a photo. But each time I must spend at least an hour standing in line surrounded by a cross-section of humanity. That hour proves most educational.

So many overweight people in the world! Why are most of my friends on the skinny side? I ask myself. *Where do all these obese people live? Who are their friends?*

And so many senior citizens! I have read about the graying of America in the news magazines, yet, again, I have few regular contacts with people outside my age range.

I am amazed at how many people wear scruffy blue jeans and cowboy boots each day, and how many have not yet discovered deodorant, and how many had no access to an orthodontist when growing up. This is the real world here in the lobby of the Driver's License Bureau. So that's who buys all those copies of *National Enquirer* each week.

My reactions may reveal my own isolation, but I suspect that all of us instinctively gravitate toward people like us and rarely step outside that circle unless something forces us to—like an order to report to the Driver's License Bureau. Or unless we meet such people at church.

I have already described how LaSalle Street Church surrounded me with people of wide diversity. As I reflect, though, I realize that every church I have attended includes a measure of diversity. I think back fondly on two people in the church of my childhood in Atlanta, Georgia—people I took turns sitting with when my mother was off teaching Sunday school. I loved sitting with Mrs. Payton because she wore animals around her neck. She had a stole, a garish bit of frippery that consisted of two minks biting each other's tails. All during the service I would play with the hard, shiny eyes, the sharp, pointed teeth, and the soft skin and floppy tails of those animals. Mrs. Payton's minks helped me endure many a wearisome sermon.

Mr. Ponce wore no animals around his neck, but I knew no kinder person anywhere. He had six children of his own, and he seemed happy only when a child was occupying his lap. He was a huge man, and I could sit there contentedly for an entire service without his leg falling asleep. He praised the pictures I drew on the church bulletin, and drew funny faces in my hands that would smile and wink when I moved my fingers a certain way.

I remember Mr. Ponce for his kindness, and also for an enormous sprout of nasal hair, easily visible when I looked up from his lap. If you had asked me then who I liked best, Mrs. Payton or Mr. Ponce, I would have had a hard time answering, but probably Mr. Ponce would get the edge. My own father died when I was only a year old, and Mr. Ponce provided for me a comforting male presence.

Later, when I grew older and more sophisticated, I learned the facts about Mrs. Payton and Mr. Ponce. Mrs. Payton was rich, which accounted for the animals around her neck. Her family owned a successful Cadillac dealership. Mr. Ponce, on the other hand, drove a garbage truck and barely brought in enough money to support his large family. When I learned these facts, I realized to my shame that as an adult I probably would not have befriended Mr. Ponce. Conversation with him would have been awkward; we might have run out of things to discuss. We probably would have shared few interests.

I am glad, very glad, that the church of Jesus Christ in my childhood included both of these friends. I now see that the church should be an environment where both Mrs. Payton of the hairy stole and Mr. Ponce of the hairy nose feel equally welcome. I should not have to wait three years for my trip to the Driver's License Bureau for a reminder of what the real world is like.

In the words of John Howard Yoder,

The church is then not simply the bearer of the message of reconciliation, in the way a newspaper or a telephone company can bear any message with which it is entrusted. Nor is the church simply the result of a message, as an alumni association is the product of a school or the crowd in a theater is the product of the reputation of the film. That men and women are called together to a new social wholeness is itself the work of God, which gives meaning to history ...

God's Emergi-Center

In recent years these mutants of the health care industry have sprouted up in residential areas, in strip malls, in city storefronts, in sites as convenient as a Seven-Eleven store. Although they go by different names, in essence they are hospital emergency rooms without the hospital. Now, instead of driving five miles to a hospital to fill out six forms in triplicate and wait in a crowded lobby for an hour while accident victims break in line ahead of you, you can drive to an Emergi-Center and have a finger stitched up, a swollen ankle examined, or a stomach ache diagnosed.

I like to think of the church as one of those Emergi-Centers: open long hours, convenient to find, willing to serve the needs of people who drop in with unexpected emergencies.

I used to bristle when I heard someone accuse Christianity of being a "crutch" religion, a faith that attracted the poor and the crippled and those who could not quite make it on their own. But the more I read the Gospels and the Prophets, the more willingly I admit to a "crutch" faith. Those who make such disdainful comments about Christianity are usually self-confident, successful over-achievers who have made it on their own by looking out for number one, without asking anyone for help.

Frankly, the gospel has little to offer people who refuse to admit need. Blessed are the poor in spirit, Jesus said, and those who mourn, and the persecuted. Basic repentance requires me to come prostrate before God and admit that God, not I, is best qualified to tell me how to live. (Perhaps for this reason Jesus singled out the wealthy as the group least likely to enter the kingdom of heaven.)

Actually, though, self-confident overachievers make up a very small proportion of this sad, pain-filled world of ours. If I pause and think about the people in my neighborhood, I encounter a whole catalog of human needs: a family devastated by a brain-damaged child, a young woman's messy affair and divorce, a homosexual's struggle against promiscuity, a diagnosis of terminal cancer, a sudden loss of job. Those needs have reached the crisis level; every one of us must contend with the normal human condition of loneliness, pride, occasional depression, fear, and alienation. Where can we take our minor scrapes and bruises, and our major fractures and gaping psychic wounds?

We can go to church. As I read the letters to the Corinthians again, I note that they contain, in addition to the strong admonitions, some of Paul's most intimate words of loving concern. I have a hunch that Paul prayed more and fussed more over that church than he did over some of the more stable congregations he left around the Mediterranean rim. Corinth was an Emergi-Center kind of church, and Paul wanted it to succeed precisely because the odds were stacked against such a cantankerous group of people.

When I think about the history of the Christian church, I view with shame and sadness much that has transpired in the name of Jesus Christ: the Inquisition,

Crusades, racial pogroms, abuse of wealth. Yet in this one area, binding human wounds, the church has done something right. In the major cities of the U.S., the names of the largest hospitals very often include a word like Baptist or Presbyterian or Methodist, or the name of a saint: St. Jude's, St. Luke's. Though many of those hospitals are no longer overtly religious, the names testify to their origins as a mission of a church that reached out tangibly to a hurting world.

Overseas, the trend is even clearer. In a country like India, where only three percent of the population call themselves Christian, nearly a third of the health care is provided by Christians. Ask an Indian to describe a Christian, and she may well describe someone who saved the life of her child or treated a member of her family. To mention one example, most of the major advances in the research and treatment of leprosy came through Christian missionaries in India. Why? For a time, only they were willing to devote their lives to work among its victims, many of them Untouchables.

We cannot all be doctors and nurses, and technologically advanced countries are taking care of health needs in other ways (such as Emergi-Centers). Even so, some human needs are still met best in the midst of a loving community like a church. It is no accident that the modern hospice movement, which cares for the terminally ill, was founded by a Christian doctor, Dame Cicely Saunders, and that the majority of hospice groups have some religious connection.

I saw a less dramatic illustration of this process at work in a suburban church I attended, a small church that was hardly distinctive. Its worship services showed little creativity, and the pastor's sermons were marginal. But to one person, Deborah Bates, that church served as a full-purpose Emergi-Center.

One day Deborah's husband abruptly moved out, leaving her with four children, a deteriorating house, and very little child support. He had found another woman, and for many months Deborah turned to members of the church for shoulders to cry on as she tried to cope with her own feelings of guilt and rejection. She had practical needs too: a leaky roof, plugged-up sewer drains, a rattle-trap car. Deborah required long-term care.

Some twenty individuals from that small congregation spent time baby-sitting, painting, repairing Deborah's house or car. One man hired her, training her in a new career. A wealthy woman offered to pay for her children's education. For at least five years Deborah limped along, propped up by the "crutch" provided by members of the church.

I imagine the motley church at Corinth often had to function as an Emergi-Center, and in fact Paul tells us of one person who found healing in the church. The apostle's first letter to the Corinthians expresses his shock and outrage at a man involved with his stepmother, "a kind [of immorality] that does not occur even among pagans" (5:1). At one point Paul was ready to hand the man over to Satan. Yet that same man, many scholars believe, makes an appearance in 2 Corinthians 2. The church had punished him and was now ready to forgive and welcome him back into the fold. Emergency treatment had proven effective.

On several occasions I had the opportunity to assist with a church communion service. The congregants came forward in groups and knelt at a prayer rail. I would break off a piece of bread, hand it to each person individually, and say, "The body of Christ, broken for you." I did not know everyone, but I knew enough to recognize in these my fellow-worshipers a need for comfort and for healing. Women like Deborah, who had been abandoned by their husbands. Judy, who sent her paycheck back to India to support her large extended family. Josh, who had found no work since leaving a printing plant over his discomfort with the pornography they were producing. Sarah, a young woman with Lou Gehrig's disease, who had to be carried to the front.

One young mother came to the communion rail with her baby sucking noisily at her breast. That provided for me a picture of the transfer of spiritual nourishment that takes place in communion. Physical nourishment flowed directly into that mother and then on to the newborn, who depended wholly on his mother for what he needed to stay alive. "The body of Christ, broken for you"—those words took on a new, profound meaning as I tore off each piece and placed it in the outstretched hand of each congregant. The church is a place where we can bring our pain, for it was founded by One whose body was broken for us, in order to give us life.

God's CTA Train

For several years I enrolled in literature courses at the University of Chicago, at the extreme south end of the city. To get there, I rode a Chicago Transit Authority elevated train some eighty-five blocks, then transferred to a local bus.

The train ride offered a sociological tour of Chicago. Where I caught the train, English was often drowned out by Spanish or Greek or Polish. As we headed toward Chicago's downtown Loop area, well-dressed Yuppies predominated. Both those groups, ethnics and Yuppies, got off before we reached the south side. There, I saw only black faces as the train threaded its way through middle-class, then lower-class, and then combat-zone areas of the city.

I started noticing the churches out the train window. Catholic churches dotted the ethnic areas, mini-cathedrals built in the European style with domes and bell towers. The African-American sections had mostly storefront churches with exotic names: Beulah Land Today Missionary Church, Holy Spirit of Brotherhood Church of God in Christ, Water in the Rock Baptist. Finally, as we approached the University of Chicago, I could see the magnificent Gothic cathedral built by the Rockefeller family.

On campus I spent my time studying such writers as T. S. Eliot, W. H. Auden, Søren Kierkegaard, John Donne, and the Japanese Christian novelist Shusako Endo. After class, I would leave those imposing gray-stone buildings and retrace my journey, starting this time in the slums and working my way back through the mosaic of neighborhoods.

Again and again I was struck with the enormous breadth of the Christian faith. It contains within it enough majesty and profundity to inspire minds like John Milton and John Donne, and Leo Tolstoy and T. S. Eliot, and to challenge agnostic graduate students who study their work to this day. Yet the gospel was entrusted, originally, to simple peasants. Very likely, some of the founders of our religion could not read or write. Jesus himself left no manuscripts for us to study.

The journey to and from the university on the CTA train captured for me two aspects of the church, and my need to learn from both. From Water in the Rock Baptist,

I learn the simple beauty of the gospel that can speak to every man and woman; I learn to seek the actual Spirit of God who is alive on this earth. At the same time, I can also encounter the mystery that an author like Kierkegaard or Endo represents, and come away humbly aware that none of us has fully figured out the message of the cross or of God's grace.

Pascal recognized this truth:

> Other religions, as the pagan, are more popular, for they consist in externals. But they are not for educated people. A purely intellectual religion would be more suited to the learned, but it would be of no use to the common people. The Christian religion alone is adapted to all, being composed of externals and internals. It raises the common people to the internal, and humbles the proud to the external; it is not perfect without the two, for the people must understand the spirit of the letter, and the learned must submit their spirit to the letter.

In the words of the apostle Paul, "God chose the foolish things of the world to shame the wise; God chose the weak things of the world to shame the strong" (1 Corinthians 1:27). Yes, and God also chose a few rare individuals like the apostle Paul himself, but even his daunting intellect proved no match for the reality of an encounter with God's own self. The church, God's church, is big enough, and small enough, to exalt the humble and humble the exalted.

God's Family

I feel secure using this image of the church, for it is one used within the Bible. I believe, though, that the vision of the church as a family has even more meaning today than in biblical times because of changes in society.

Read the book of Genesis, and you read a history of families. It begins with Adam and Eve's family, with one good son and one bad. Keep reading and you encounter Abraham's family, which took decades to get off the ground. Then follows the story of Isaac's family, and Jacob's. Everything else flows out of Jacob's family, for the Old Testament records the history of "the children of Israel," Jacob's new name.

Contrast that approach with any modern textbook of history, which tells of the rise and fall of civilizations. In contemporary newspapers we read of nations and cities and universities and government agencies and companies. The focus has shifted from families to institutions. Yet the New Testament stubbornly presents the church as being more like a family than an institution.

Institutions are based upon, and held together by, status and rank. A soldier in the Army knows exactly where he or she stands, and everyone else knows too; stripes on a uniform announce the rank. Competitive ranking begins with the A's, B's, C's, and F's of the first grade. In the business world, title, salary, and other "perks" signify status. You can ride an elevator floor by floor up the World Trade Center in New York and, just by observing the office furniture, see the status of the executives rise with the height of the building.

In an institution, status derives from performance. The business world has learned that human beings respond well to rewards of status; they can be powerful motivators. In families, however, status works differently. How does one earn status in a family? A child "earns" the family's rights solely by virtue of birth. An underachieving child is not kicked out of the family. Indeed, a sickly child, who "produces" very little, may actually receive more attention than her healthy siblings. As novelist John Updike once wrote, "Families teach us how love exists in a realm beyond liking or disliking, coexisting with indifference, rivalry, and even antipathy."

Similarly, in God's family, we are plainly told, "there is neither Jew nor Greek, male nor female, slave nor free." All such artificial distinctions have melted under the sun of God's grace. As God's adopted children we gain the same rights, clearly undeserved, as those enjoyed by the firstborn, Jesus Christ himself — a book like Ephesians underscores that astonishing truth again and again.

For this reason, it grieves me to see local churches that run more like a business institution than a family. In his discussion of spiritual gifts, the apostle Paul warns sternly against valuing one member more highly than another.

> The eye cannot say to the hand, "I don't need you!" And the head cannot say to the feet, "I don't need you!" On the contrary, those parts of the body that seem to be weaker are indispensable, and the parts that we think are less honorable we treat with special honor. And the parts that are unpresentable are treated with special modesty, while our presentable parts need no special treatment. But God has combined the members of the body and has given greater honor to the parts that lacked it, so that there should be no division in the body, but that its parts should have equal concern for each other. If one part suffers, every part suffers with it; if one part is honored, every part rejoices with it. (1 Corinthians 12:21–26)

In this passage Paul is drawing on his favorite metaphor for the church: the human body. And yet the best way I can visualize how these truths might play themselves out in an actual group of people is to go back to a scene of a human family gathered around a table for a holiday meal.

Every family contains some successful individuals and some miserable failures. At Thanksgiving, corporate vice-president Aunt Mary sits next to Uncle Charles, who drinks too much and has never held a job. Although some of the folks gathered around the table are clever and some stupid, some are ugly and some attractive, some healthy and some disabled, in a family these differences become insignificant. Cousin Johnny seems to try his best to alienate himself from the family, but there is no practical way to drum him out. He belongs, like all of us, because we were born of the same ancestors and the same genes coil inside our cells. Failure does not cancel out membership. A family, said Robert Frost, "is the place where, when you have to go there, they have to take you in."

I sometimes think that God invented the human institution of the family as a training ground to prepare us for how we should relate within other institutions. Families work best not by papering over their differences but rather by celebrating them. A healthy family builds up the weakest members while not tearing down the strong. As John Wesley's mother put it, "Which child of mine do I love best? I love the sick one until he's well, the one away from home until she's back."

Family is the one human institution we have no choice over. We get in simply by being born, and as a result we are involuntarily thrown together with a menagerie of strange and unlike people. Church calls for another step: to voluntarily choose to band together with a strange menagerie because of a common bond in Jesus

Christ. I have found that such a community more resembles a family than any other human institution. Henri Nouwen once defined a community as "a place where the person you least want to live with always lives." His definition applies equally to the group that gathers each Thanksgiving and the group that congregates each Sunday morning.

God's Locker Room

For most of the year, I win the battle against TV addiction. As I have written elsewhere, though, I must confess that just before springtime a mysterious force known as "March Madness" draws me toward an annual televised rite: the NCAA College Basketball Tournament. I cannot resist the temptation to tune in.

No one should have to endure the kind of pressure these young athletes face. At the age of nineteen or twenty, they perform before thirty million television viewers with the entire weight of the university, state, and their professional careers riding on every dribble and rebound. The crucial game of the Final Four manages to tighten up in the last few minutes, and the season always seems to come down to one eighteen-year-old kid standing on the free throw line with one second left on the clock.

He approaches the free throw line and dribbles the ball nervously. At the last possible instant, the opposing team calls time out, to rattle him.

For the next two minutes the free throw shooter squats on the sidelines, listening to his coach, trying not to think about what all twenty thousand fans are screaming about: his upcoming basketball shot. His teammates pat him encouragingly, but say nothing. He has shot a hundred thousand practice free throws over the season, making three-fourths of them. But this free throw is different.

If he makes it, he will be the hero of all heroes on campus. His picture will be on the front page. He could virtually run for governor. If he fails, he will be the goat of all goats. How can he face his teammates again? How can he face life? Twenty years from now he'll be sitting in a counselor's office, tracing all his problems back to this decisive moment. He returns to the free throw line with the tension of a whole career etched in the lines of his face.

One year, I remember, I left the room to answer a phone call just as the kid was setting himself to shoot. Worry lines creased his forehead. He was biting his lower lip. His left leg quivered at the knee. Twenty thousand fans were yelling, waving banners and handkerchiefs to distract him.

The phone call took longer than expected, and when I returned I saw a new sight. This same kid, his hair drenched with Gatorade, was now riding atop the shoulders of his teammates, cutting the cords of a basketball net. He had not a care in the world. His grin filled the entire screen. He made the shot!

Those two freeze-frames—the same kid crouching at the free throw line and then celebrating on his friend's shoulders—came to symbolize for me the difference between law and grace. Under law, my destiny rides on everything that I do. To please the crowd, the coach, the pro scouts—to please God—I have to make the shot. My eternity depends on it. If I miss, it will sear me forever. I have to make it. I cannot fail.

Jesus' kingdom calls us to another way, one that depends not on our performance but his own. We do not have to achieve but merely follow Jesus. He has already earned for us the costly victory of God's acceptance. As a result, church should not be one more place for me to compete and get a performance rating. Like a victorious locker room, church is a place to exult, to give thanks, to celebrate the great news that all is forgiven, that God is love, that victory is certain. Church is a beacon of grace to the rest of the world, not a fortress of legalism.

That is the church as described in the Bible, at least.

One Final Metaphor

As I let my mind roam over various metaphors to describe the church today, I find many other possibilities.

The church is God's welfare office, an institution set up to heal the blind, set free the captive, feed the hungry, and bring Good News to the poor — the original mandate Jesus proclaimed.

The church is God's neighborhood bar, a hangout like the television show *Cheers* for people who know all about your lousy boss, your mother with heart trouble back in North Carolina, and the teenager who won't do what you tell him; a place where you can unwind, spill your life story, and get a sympathetic look, not a self-righteous leer.

After trying out these and other metaphors, I find myself returning time after time to the one Paul settled on as most accurate and appropriate: the church as Christ's body. Chapters 12–14 of 1 Corinthians adumbrate the theme that will appear in the later Epistles. "The body is a unit," Paul says, "though it is made up of many parts; and though all its parts are many, they form one body" (12:12). An eye, a hand, a kidney, a foot, a nose — the body works only by balancing the polar forces of unity and diversity, by bringing together people of all shapes and sizes who are nevertheless made one in Christ Jesus.

I dare not start in on all the analogies that flow from that one great image, for I have collaborated with Dr. Paul Brand in two books on this very subject (*Fearfully and Wonderfully Made* and *In His Image*). To me, the most important lesson from the body is this: we—you and I—form the primary representation of God's presence in the world.

What is God like? Where does God live? How can the world get to know God? God's Presence no longer dwells in a tabernacle in the Sinai, or in a temple in Jerusalem. God has chosen instead to dwell in ordinary, even ornery, people like you and me. My pastor in Colorado has a witty response that underscores this point. When someone says to him, "What a beautiful church!" he replies, "Why thank you. I have been dieting—glad you noticed." His point: God's church consists of *people*, not buildings in places like Colorado or Chicago.

As I look around on Sunday morning at the people populating the pews, I see the risk that God has assumed. For whatever reason, God now reveals himself in the world not through a pillar of smoke and fire, not even through the physical body of his Son in Galilee, but through the mongrel collection that comprises my local church and every other such gathering in God's name.

In this confused and confusing world, we are called to share in the representation of what God is like, to give God form in this world. Martin Luther called us "God's masks": because the world cannot withstand the direct force of God's glory, he said, God uses human beings as the prime expression of himself.

The Apostle Paul never seemed to get over the shock

of that truth. He took the mundane issues at Corinth so seriously because he believed they reflected not only on Corinth but on God. For the watching world, we ourselves offer up proof that God is alive. We form the visible shape of what God is like.

When I look at that shape around me, I easily get discouraged, because much of the time we give a very poor representation of what God is like. And yet when I turn to a book like 1 Corinthians, I feel a sudden gust of hope. To whom was Paul writing those soaring words of chapters 12–14? To that motley crew of Corinthians—idolaters, adulterers, scandalmongers, and the like.

No church I know of today fulfills the promise of all the metaphors I have mentioned here. Yet every church represents that promise and offers a whisper of hope. Imperfectly, to be sure, we all reveal some aspect of the shape of God's body. How does God view the church that gives such a distorted image? Perhaps, as Malcolm Muggeridge suggests, "as God has looked at His creatures through the aeons: disappointment without end weighed against inexhaustible love."

We humans cause God great pain, yet God remains passionately involved with us. Should not I have something of that same attitude toward the church around me?

CHAPTER 3

REACHING BEYOND
THE WALLS

It is not what you are nor what you have been that
God sees with his all-merciful eyes, but what you
desire to be.

THE CLOUD OF UNKNOWING

In one of his parables Søren Kierkegaard tells of a church attended by a flock of domesticated geese. Every week they waddled in and listened to the preacher hold forth on the wonders of flight. "We don't have to walk on the ground and stay in this place," the gander exhorted them. "We can lift ourselves into the air and soar to distant regions, more blessed climes. We can fly!" And after hearing the sermon, every week the geese quacked "Amen!" and then filed out the door and waddled home to their own affairs. All they had to do was flap their wings.

Frankly, many churches do not come close to fulfilling the lofty promise suggested by the metaphors of the previous chapter. They operate like private clubs, designed for the benefit of members, whereas the New Testament holds up the model of a church whose activities exist primarily for the sake of outsiders. What keeps us from becoming the church God had in mind?

I have watched a pattern time and again: a church starts off with high ideals, generates a flurry of activity, and then gradually tempers its vision, settling for something far less than ideal. When I stood outside the church looking in, I found much to criticize. But once I fully entered the church, I realized the difficulty in sustaining anything like the New Testament vision of what the church should be. I have much more sympathy for the church's failures now that I am contributing to them! Church "frustrates us into holiness," says Richard Rohr, by holding up a shining vision and then inviting us to join the lackluster reality.

Indeed, I experience a personal pattern of lowered ideals whenever I get involved in ministry activity. I start strong, hit a wall of fatigue and discouragement, and am tempted to give up. Ministry involves stress and personal sacrifice that can wear down even the most committed workers. It may be more blessed to give than to receive, but it is also more draining.

We are all called to do the work of ministry. Unless we understand the nature of the challenge, though—the "occupational hazards" of ministry—we in the church will inevitably retrench, scaling back our mission to serve ourselves, not the world. When we do so, we become just like every other human institution and the church's unique calling fades away.

As I watch Christians active in ministry and reflect on my own experience, I observe a precarious balance between hypersensitivity and emotional callus. Some workers remain so hypersensitive to the pain around them that they succumb to that pain. Others develop a callousness that makes ministry seem like just another job, a demanding volunteer assignment with few rewards. Neither group lasts long in doing the work of the church. I gained new insight into this process within the Body of

Christ when I began to look at a similar process at work within my own body—specifically, my left foot.

My Bunion

I have a bunion, a deformity related to the bone structure of my foot. The big toes of most people stick out straight or slant in toward the other toes at a gentle fifteen-degree angle. On my left foot (the right one has been surgically corrected), the big toe juts in at a totally unacceptable forty-degree angle, jamming the smaller toes together. As tendons shrink further, this toe will wrap itself across the top of its neighbor and I'll have to submit my left foot to the surgeon's knife as well.

As the toe has angled in, an ungainly bump has developed on the side of the foot: my bunion. This bony defect sometimes causes pain, and it always complicates shoe-buying. Shoe manufacturers, I have learned, do not tend to make shoes with large, ungainly bumps on the side. As a result, I must buy shoes that are too large for my right (surgically corrected) foot, and trust the bunion to impose its own shape on the left shoe. It always obliges, at a price.

A jogger for more than twenty years, I have learned the sequence of my body's adaptation to shoes all too well. As I run, my left foot detects the lack of support along its big toe, angling as it does away from the shoe cushion, and ingeniously it decides to create its own support to fill in the gap. First I develop a blister, a temporary, liquid-filled pad that sorely complicates the act of running. When I persist, the foot produces a more permanent modification comprising thick layers of hardened keratin: a callus. Over time, the callus fills the gap in the shoe, and I run in comfort—for a while.

Eventually the callus grows so large that it creates friction of its own, and painful blood blisters form underneath the callus. I pull out a manicure kit and trim the callus until I reach layers of tender pink skin underneath, and then the process begins to re-cycle.

I used to resent my bunion, harboring hostility as the callus developed, in anticipation of the tenderness to follow. Then one day Dr. Paul Brand, my coauthor on three books on the human body, helped to soften my attitude. This is what he told me.

"I once had a similar problem. One year in medical school I spent the summer sailing on a schooner on the North Sea. The first week, as I yanked on heavy ropes to hoist the sail, my fingertips became so sore that they bled and kept me awake at night with the pain. By the end of the second week calluses were forming, and soon afterwards thick calluses covered my fingers. I had no more trouble with tenderness that summer—the calluses protected me. But when I returned to medical school two months later, I found to my chagrin that I had lost my finer skills in dissection. The calluses made my fingers less sensitive and now I could scarcely feel the instruments. For a few weeks I worried that I had ruined my career as a surgeon. Gradually, though, the calluses disappeared in response to my sedentary life, and sensitivity returned. Each time, my body was loyally finding ways to adapt to the changing needs I imposed on it."

I began to see that my body is struggling constantly to find the proper balance between hypersensitivity and callus. Like Dr. Brand's fingers, my foot loses sensitivity to pain and pressure when it builds up the calluses. It does so willingly for a time, as an accommodation to my jogging. But after a while the wisdom of the body determines that it dare not make my foot too callused. To persuade me to stop abusing my foot, my body creates blood blisters, which make me hypersensitive to pain and force adjustments in my behavior.

Ever since, I have tried to view my body's efforts with gratitude, not resentment. I understand that sometimes my actions call for hypersensitivity and sometimes for callus. I cannot say that I *enjoy* the routine of blister/callus/blood blister/manicure. Yet I now grasp the reason behind it, and I appreciate my body's attempts to cope.

My conversation with Dr. Brand did something else as well: it gave me a useful insight into ministry in the Body of Christ. As the "skin" on the Body, people doing ministry expose themselves to changing stresses. Sometimes a person in ministry needs the fine skill of a surgeon, for the repair of human souls can require more sensitivity than the repair of human bodies. At other times the person in ministry, overburdened, short of resources, besieged by unsolvable problems, needs a layer of callus. Indeed, at times ministry closely resembles what a sailor endures as he clings to the lines of the mainsail in the midst of a raging storm.

Christian ministry, like my foot, like Dr. Brand's fingertips, dangles on a pendulum between hypersensitivity and callus.

Eating Tears

My idea was pretty simple at the beginning. I started to volunteer in wards with terminally ill children or burn victims—just go in there to cheer them up a little, spread around some giggles. Gradually, it developed that I was going to come in as a clown.

First, somebody gave me a red rubber nose, and I put that to work. Then I started doing some elementary makeup. Then I got a yellow, red, and green clown suit. Finally, some nifty, tremendous wing-tip shoes, about two and a half feet long, with green tips and heels, white in the middle. They came from a clown who was retiring and wanted his feet to keep on walking.

[Things] were very tough for me at the beginning—very. You see some pretty terrible things in these wards. Seeing children dying or mutilated is nothing most of us ever get prepared for. Nobody teaches us to face suffering in this society. We never talk about it until we get hit in the face....

Some of us were setting up to show *Godzilla* in the kids' leukemia ward. I was making up kids as clowns. One kid was totally bald from chemotherapy, and when I finished doing his face, another kid said, "Go on and do the rest of his head." The kid loved the idea. And when I was done, his sister said, "Hey, we can show the movie on Billy's head." And he really loved that idea. So we set up *Godzilla* and ran it on Billy's head, and Billy was pleased as punch, and we were all mighty proud of Billy. It was quite a moment. Especially when the doctors arrived....

Burnt skin or bald heads on little kids—what do you do? I guess you just face it—when the kids are really hurting so bad, and so afraid, and probably dying, and everybody's heart is breaking. Face it, and see what happens after that, see what to do next.

I got the idea of traveling with popcorn. When a kid is crying I dab up the tears with the popcorn and pop it into my mouth or into his or hers. We sit around together and eat the tears. (From *How Can I Help?* by Ram Dass and Paul Gorman)

In ministry, hypersensitivity means, quite simply, feeling someone else's pain. It means eating another person's tears.

I have clear memories of sitting at the dining table in our apartment in Chicago, eating tears. Janet would tell me about George, in a Cook County Hospital ward being treated for gangrene from frostbite. Because he had no permanent place to sleep, often he ended up outdoors. One night he slept with too little protection, and the Chicago cold got to him. A few days later, a senior citizen noticed that George was missing, and after many phone calls Janet tracked him down.

Janet felt helpless before the huge social problems of homelessness, violent crime, and inadequate health care. She did what she could during the day but sometimes, in the evening, all she could do was cry. Several times, especially after one of the senior citizens had died, Janet said something like this. "I should resign. I'm no good at this job. Look at me, sitting here bawling over one of my 'clients.' It's not professional. I can't handle the pain."

I would reply, "Janet, you are the only person in the entire world who is shedding a tear because Paul died. Do you really think those senior citizens would be better served by someone who did not cry?"

After we moved to Colorado, Janet worked as a chaplain in a hospice run by an Orthodox order. Forty-five people died there every month, which meant that almost every day Janet went to work, someone died. We ate more tears.

Does it do any good, this eating of tears? Does it help for a person to be hypersensitive, to deliberately risk exposure to another person's pain? Yes, I believe that it does. I believe that it helps when a man puts on a red rubber nose and slips into oversized shoes to bring joy and laughter to a kids' leukemia ward, and when that man stays to eat tear-laced popcorn. And I believe that it mattered a great deal to George to know that one person—maybe only one person—bore his pain and carried it home with her.

Henri Nouwen's slim book with the wonderful title *The Wounded Healer* describes lonely, abandoned people who have no one to love them. Nouwen tells of a young minister who has nothing to offer an old man facing surgery except his own loving concern. "No man can stay alive when nobody is waiting for him," writes Nouwen. "Everyone who returns from a long and difficult trip is looking for someone waiting for him at the station or the airport. Everyone wants to tell his story and share his moments of pain and exhilaration with someone who stayed home, waiting for him to come back."

Sometimes the only meaning those of us in ministry can offer suffering people is the assurance that their suffering, which has no apparent meaning for them, has meaning for us.

Nourished by Tears

At times, though, despite our best efforts to honor others' pain, we encounter suffering that appears utterly devoid of meaning. At those times the eating of tears may seem useless. I am thinking of a man with Alzheimer's disease: his daughter tries to attend to his needs, but every day her heart is broken by the sad shell of what used to be her father.

Or I think of a severely disabled child with an IQ in the 30–40 range. The child may live a long life lying motionless in a crib, unable to talk, unable to comprehend, soaking up expensive professional care.

Where is there meaning in such a senile adult and in such a child? What is the purpose of sharing their tears? I have received help in answering this question from a doctor in Eastern Germany. For many years the church there, restricted in their activities by the former Communist government, adopted the least "valuable" or "useful" members of society.

"What is the point of their lives? Do their lives have any meaning?" asked Dr. Jurgen Trogisch, a pediatrician who devoted himself to severely mentally handicapped children.

For a long time Dr. Trogisch could not answer the question of meaning. He went ahead and performed his medical tasks, but he had no answer. Then he conducted an introductory course to train new helpers for the center. At the end of the one-year training period, he asked these young helpers to fill out a survey. Among the questions was this one, "What changes have taken place in your life since you became totally involved with disabled people?" Here is a selection of their answers:

- For the first time in my life I feel I am doing something really significant.
- I feel I can now do things I wouldn't have thought myself capable of before.
- During my time here I have won the affection of Sabine. Having had the opportunity to involve myself with a disabled person, I no longer think of her as disabled at all.
- I am more responsive now to human suffering and it arouses in me the desire to help.
- It's made me question what is really important in life.

- Work has assumed a new meaning and purpose. I feel I'm needed now.
- I've learned to be patient and to appreciate even the slightest sign of progress.
- In observing the disabled, I've discovered myself.
- I've become more tolerant. My own little problems don't seem so important any longer, and I've learned to accept myself with all my inadequacies. Above all I've learned to appreciate the little pleasures of life, and especially I thank God that he has shown me that love can achieve more than hate or force.

As Dr. Trogisch read their responses, he realized with a start the answer to his question. The meaning of the suffering of those children was being worked out in the lives of others, his helpers, who were learning lessons that no sophisticated educational system could teach. Where else could teenagers and college students learn such inestimable lessons as these?

Dr. Trogisch has put his finger on a by-product of the church's mission that often gets overlooked. We tend to focus on the *objects* of ministry: the souls led to Christ, the marriages rescued, the poor fed and housed, the homebound elderly visited, the teenagers challenged. Yet as I read the New Testament, Jesus seems equally interested in what effect ministry is having on the people who are doing the work of ministry themselves.

When seventy-two disciples came back with exciting reports of grand results, Jesus celebrated with them for a moment and then said, "However, do not rejoice that the spirits submit to you, but rejoice that your names are written in heaven." Evidently, what was happening inside the disciples was as important to Jesus as anything they had accomplished on the outside.

Eating tears benefits the one who voluntarily takes them on, as well as the one who sheds them in the first place. As an introvert, I usually have to force myself to volunteer in some helping capacity. I have to screw up my courage to head to a shelter to fix Thanksgiving dinner, or to make a hospital visit. Yet without exception, whenever I do so I find that I benefit. I come away enriched by characters I meet, stirred by their stories, amazed at human resiliency. I return to my mostly solitary occupation with a new sense of thanksgiving and a renewed commitment to serve others in what little way I can. I have experienced firsthand the salutary effect of shared tears.

Strength through Weakness

Paradoxically, when a church avoids ministry because of the pain and complications it may bring, the church itself suffers. It remains stunted, and does not mature.

Jesus gave us a model for the work of the church at the Last Supper. While his disciples kept proposing more organization—Hey, let's elect officers, establish a hierarchy, set standards of professionalism—Jesus quietly picked up a towel and basin of water and began to wash their feet. "I have set you an example that you should do as I have done for you," he said (John 13:15). I have come to recognize this spirit of service as the single greatest hallmark of a church doing the will of God.

Buildings, facilities, a board well stocked with shrewd businessmen—these may all make a church run smoothly, but the underlying question is: What is it running smoothly *for?* I look for a congregation that fosters the quality of hypersensitivity to pain. Whereas the rest of us turn our faces from the homeless, then shake our heads and get on with our lives, servants say, No, we cannot turn away from this pain. Homeless people bear God's image too. We must serve them, as Jesus would—as if they were Jesus.

Reflecting on Jesus' style of ministry, Paul said, "Your attitude should be the same as that of Christ Jesus: Who ... made himself nothing, taking the very nature of a servant ..." (Philippians 2:5–7). The biblical pattern for ministry recognizes that the path to strength proceeds through weakness.

Paul himself pled three times for his "thorn in the flesh" to be removed, and we can only speculate on the content of those prayers. *Lord, think how much more effective I would be if you removed this thorn. It's holding me back in my ministry. It's inhibiting your work. I could accomplish great things if you healed this problem and let me regain my strength.* The answer to the apostle's prayers was a firm negative.

Why did God allow Paul's suffering to continue? The apostle himself gives the blunt reason: "To keep me from becoming conceited." God had said to him, "My power is made perfect in weakness." And Paul learned to respond, "Therefore I will boast all the more gladly about my weaknesses, so that Christ's power may rest in me. That is why, for Christ's sake, I delight in weaknesses, in insults, in hardships, in persecutions, in difficulties. For when I am weak, then I am strong" (2 Corinthians 12:7–10).

At twelve-step groups I have heard wrenching stories of what it takes for a person to learn to confront his or her own brokenness, to "reach the end of myself," as they often put it. Alcoholics tell of an excruciating process that must play itself out before they can admit they are weak, not strong, and must permanently depend on a Higher Power as a source of outside strength. There is an easier way to learn these lessons, I have found: volunteer in some ministry arm of the church.

I have seen in my own wife the direct and personal benefits of ministry. She went to a poorly furnished office each day and spent her time among people who rarely said "thank you." She had to raise her own salary, a procedure that replayed her missionary kid's shame. But I can truthfully say that her willingness to expose herself to others' pain ended up nourishing her as much as them. With all the objectivity a husband can muster, I see her now as a stronger, more beautiful person. She received few rewards for her work, as the world measures them. The rewards worked themselves out inside her.

Those who minister have an opportunity to learn compassion (the very word means "to suffer with"), humility, patience, and other such qualities that would never even make the agenda at most Fortune 500 firms. We dare not discount the rewards that God grants. They are precious to God, and more valuable than any amount of money and prestige one can accumulate in other professions. Jesus' most often-repeated declaration in the Gospels is that we find our lives by losing them. We lose them best in service to others.

Hypersensitivity to pain can be a resource, an unexpected gift. The same tears that break our hearts may also nourish us in ways that matter most to God.

A Callus to Cushion the Pain

One year I decided to run the Chicago Marathon. I was already running twenty to twenty-five miles a week, but my running magazines informed me I would need to double that distance to train for a marathon. In typical straight-ahead fashion, I doubled my mileage right away. I was encouraged to find that my body could manage the extra rigor. My lungs held up, my heart met the challenge, and my muscles, though sore, soon adapted. But not my bunion.

After a few weeks of the new regimen, the skin around my big toe became so hypersensitive that I could hardly walk a block, much less run ten miles. I had to cut back on exercise until gradually, painstakingly, new layers of callus built up to cope with the added stress.

Something similar happens to people in ministry. Compassionate people who are adept at serving others may suddenly enter a whole new level of stress—a friend comes down with AIDS, a spouse files for divorce, the church rumor mill shifts into high gear—and find themselves unprotected. Hypersensitivity, once their greatest strength, now becomes an enemy. The skin tissue on my foot responded by breaking down, essentially crippling me until I produced more callus, and that is also what happens to those who minister. The pain that once nourished suddenly imperils. Eat too many tears, and you get salt poisoning.

A film from the 1970s, *Resurrection*, gives a powerful image of what can happen to wounded healers. The leading character, played by Ellen Burstyn, somehow gains the gift of miraculous healing after an automobile accident. She has no religious faith to speak of and cannot explain her new powers. "Let me tell you what happens," she says to the throng of sick people who soon crowd around her. "I see the person in front of me sick, hurting, scared. Don't ask me how, but I feel them. It's like I become sick, hurting, scared. I kind of become them.... I don't know where the power comes from, just that it does come."

In one extraordinary scene, Burstyn goes to the California Institute of Psychology to have her powers investigated. In an auditorium full of psychologists and scientists, researchers roll out a hospital bed on which lies a young woman with a spastic muscle disorder. Burstyn approaches the twitching woman, hesitates, then climbs onto the bed beside her.

In a few minutes Burstyn, the healer, begins shaking. Her face distorts, her legs turn inward, her hands form rigid claws. Literally, Burstyn takes on the affliction in her own body, simultaneously releasing it from the other woman. The patient walks out, her limbs supple; Ellyn Burstyn is wheeled into a hospital room for observation.

In the movie, Ellyn Burstyn's career as a healer is short-lived because the transferred pain takes too great a toll on her. She moves to a small town in the Nevada desert and pumps gas for the few travelers who wander by, none of whom know of her miraculous powers.

How can we keep wounded healers from becoming mortally wounded healers? Realistically, can we devote ourselves to others' pain without harming ourselves? Or, to rephrase the question in terms of my bunion analogy, how can we gauge when people involved in helping others need more protective layers of callus?

I confess that I am no expert on these matters. As a borderline "type A" personality, I lack good judgment on symptoms of burnout in myself and must rely on the counsel of my wife and a few trusted friends. By being married to a person on the front lines of ministry, however, I have learned a few principles that may help others detect early symptoms of tissue breakdown. I present them as a kind of checklist of danger signs.

1) Am I more concerned about a person's pain than the person himself/herself? I once heard someone describe a nurse as, "Typhoid Mary disguised as Florence Nightingale," explaining, "She has a nonstop 'gotta help' complex. She's obsessed about relieving other people's pain because of the discomfort *she* feels about pain. As a result, she spreads around as much distress as healing."

I have learned to recognize one early warning symptom of burnout: a feeling of overwhelming personal responsibility, as though the fate of a church, a community, a nation, yea, even the entire universe rests on the shoulder of one dedicated helper.

Eugene Peterson draws a contrast between Augustine and Pelagius, two fourth-century theological opponents. Pelagius was urbane, courteous, convincing, and liked by everyone. Augustine squandered away his youth in immorality, had a strange relationship with his mother, and made many enemies. Yet Augustine started from God's grace and got it right, whereas Pelagius started from human effort and got it wrong. Augustine passionately pursued God; Pelagius methodically worked to please God. Augustine desperately needed God, and he knew it. Peterson goes on to say that Christians tend to be Augustinian in theory but Pelagian in practice. They rely on their own frenzied efforts: committee meetings, guilt-driven overtime, obsessive attempts to "fix" other people's problems.

Ministering to people in need sometimes calls instead for a sense of detachment, an appropriate callus that cushions the helper from the pain of the one who needs help. Author Frederick Buechner describes how he learned this lesson in *Telling Secrets:*

Love your neighbor as yourself is part of the great commandment. The other way to say it is, Love yourself as your neighbor. Love yourself not in some ego-centric, self-serving sense but love yourself the way you would love your friend in the sense of taking care of yourself, nourishing yourself, trying to understand, comfort, strengthen yourself. Ministers in particular, people in the caring professions in general, are famous for neglecting their selves with the result that they are apt to become in their own way as helpless and crippled as the people they are trying to care for and thus no longer selves who can be of much use to anybody. If your daughter is struggling for life in a raging torrent, you do not save her by jumping into the torrent with her, which leads only to your both drowning together. Instead you keep your feet on the dry bank—you maintain as best you can your own inner peace, the best and strongest of who you are—and from that solid ground reach out a rescuing hand. "Mind your own business" means butt out of other people's lives because in the long run they must live their lives for themselves, but it also means pay mind to your own life, your own health and wholeness, both for your own sake and ultimately for the sake of those you love too. Take care of yourself so you can take care of them. A bleeding heart is of no help to anybody if it bleeds to death.

Then Buechner, who has been writing autobiographically about his daughter, adds this sentence, "How easy it was to write such words and how impossible it was to live them."

Buechner's only salvation was that his daughter sought treatment for her life-threatening anorexia some three thousand miles from home. He was not present to "protect" her by manipulating events on her behalf. The people who were there—the doctors, nurses, social workers, and even a judge who hospitalized her against her will—had a kind of callus that Buechner the father did not have, could not have. "Those men and women were not haggard, dithering, lovesick as I was. They were realistic, tough, conscientious, and in those ways, though they would never have put it in such terms themselves, loved her in a sense that I believe is closer to what Jesus meant by love than what I had been doing."

The syndrome of unhealthy self-sacrifice for the sake of others, of bearing more of a person's pain than the person herself, is sometimes called a "savior complex." Ironically, the true Savior seemed remarkably free of such a complex. He caught a boat to escape crowds; he insisted on privacy and time alone; he accepted a "wasteful" gift of perfume that, as Judas pointed out, could have been sold, with the proceeds used to alleviate human misery.

Jesus healed everyone who asked him, but not everyone he met. He had the amazing, and rare, capacity to let people choose their own pain. He exposed Judas but did not try to prevent his evil deed; he denounced the Pharisees without trying to coerce them into his point of view; he answered a wealthy man's question with uncompromising words and let him walk away. Mark pointedly adds this comment about the wealthy man who rejected Jesus' advice, "Jesus looked at him and loved him" (Mark 10:21).

In short, Jesus showed an incredible respect for human freedom. He had no compulsion to convert the entire world in his lifetime or to cure people unready to be cured. Those of us in ministry need the kind of "Savior complex" that Jesus demonstrated.

While living among missionaries in Peru, Henri Nouwen concluded that the two most damaging motives among ministers are guilt and the desire to save. "The problem with guilt," he observed, "is that it is not taken away by work.... Guilt has roots deeper than can be reached through acts of service. On the other hand, the desire to save people from sin, from poverty, or from exploitation can be just as harmful, because the harder one tries the more one is confronted with one's own limitations. Many hardworking men and women have seen the situation getting worse during their missionary career; and if they depended solely on the success of their work, they would quickly lose their sense of self-worth."

Nouwen concludes, "When we can come to realize that our guilt has been taken away and that only God saves, then we are free to serve, then we can live truly humble lives." God works best through those who have a spirit of humility and gratitude.

Hypersensitivity to pain can be a gift, yes; but like many other gifts, if allowed to control and dominate, it can destroy. I get worried when I see helpers looking more pained and needy than the people they are helping. In the words of poet John Donne, "Other men's crosses are not my cross."

2) Do I have a community of people around me who value what I do? I once spent some time at a support facility for the Wycliffe Bible Translators in the desert near Tucson, Arizona. As is my custom I went jogging, though earlier in the morning than usual, to avoid the hot sun. Wary of rattlesnakes and scorpions I kept an anxious eye on the path. One morning, two miles down the road from Wycliffe, I looked up to see the elaborate headquarters of a nationally famous spa, an exclusive clinic for people with eating disorders and overweight people. At first I thought I had stumbled on a five-star resort. The facility, frequented by movie stars and athletes, featured swimming pools, jogging paths, basketball and tennis courts, horse trails, and shady picnic grounds. Its modern stucco buildings gleamed in the sunlight.

I could not help comparing the spa facilities to the Wycliffe base, where office buildings were functional, with little architectural embellishment, and made of concrete block. Many of the staff members lived in mobile homes scattered among the hills. It struck me that the contrast between the two facilities illustrated an inescapable fact of ministry: the world values the material more than the spiritual. In order to lose fat cells, people will pay thousands of dollars and insist on first-class treatment. Meanwhile, those called to Jesus' far more difficult campaign of rooting out problems like pride, greed, lust, violence, envy, and injustice must struggle to survive.

Fortunately, as I found out over the next few days, the Wycliffe personnel managed to maintain a high morale. The reason, I believe, is that they formed for each other a community of mutual support. The world may value cure of bodies more than cure of souls, but not these missionaries. They prayed together, worshiped together, and honored each other for the noble calling they held in common.

Many local pastors, I know, lack such a community. As one pastor told me, "I get the feeling that nobody values me. The church budget committee is always looking for ways to cut expenses, and my 'perks' seem an easy target. Honor my work? This congregation specializes in criticizing it."

People in ministry can counteract such feelings with the help of a support group that functions as a community. You can see the difference a community makes by comparing two novels, *Catch–22* and *MASH*. In the first, Joseph Heller's war novel, a paranoid-schizophrenic airman concludes the world is against him and edges toward absurdist despair. The characters who populate *MASH* (an acronym for Mobile Army Surgical Hospital) face many of the same problems, but somehow in the hills of Korea a wacky but mutually supportive community has taken shape. When choppers full of wounded descend, the doctors and nurses grimace, crack a few jokes, then pick up the tools and get to work.

Developing a community that can transform a Catch–22 setting into MASH may be the key to survival for a difficult ministry. "I would very much like to know how many fleas are tormenting my brothers at night," said Ignatius Loyola, indicating the close ties within the Jesuit order.

Occasionally a parishioner will take the initiative in looking out for the welfare of ministry staff. A wealthy couple at LaSalle Street Church, for example, sensed the need to "honor" those in ministry. One year they donated a thousand dollars for a Christmas celebration, letting the staff members decide how to spend it. The staff opted for dinner at a plush Chicago restaurant and tickets to the Second City comedy club. I tagged along as the spouse of a staff member, and I could read in the faces around me how much the evening meant to people who rarely had the opportunity—or resources—for a night out on the town. All over the city, big corporations were throwing holiday bashes for employees. Yet how many churches or ministries had provided a memorable way to honor their faithful representatives?

My wife ministered among some of the poorest people

in Chicago, and the suffering and injustice she encountered each day were nearly overwhelming. I soon found that it was up to me to detect when Janet needed a weekend away or a dinner out or a Chicago Symphony Orchestra concert. She felt guilty indulging in such luxuries — none of the senior citizens she worked with could afford them — but I knew that a steady diet of pain would render her incapable of helping anyone. As part of her support community, I had to help provide for her the inner nourishment that gave her strength to continue on the front lines.

3) Am I confusing God with life? I got that phrase from a man named Douglas, whom I interviewed while researching the book *Disappointment with God*. Of all the people I knew, Douglas had lived the most Job-like existence. Just when he made a sacrificial decision to enter urban ministry, his world unraveled. Funding for his ministry fell through, his wife got cancer, and a drunk driver hit his car, badly injuring Douglas and his twelve-year-old daughter. Not long afterward, his wife died. I wanted Douglas to describe his disappointment with God, but to my surprise he reported that he had not had such feelings.

"I learned a long time ago, and especially through these tragedies," Douglas told me, "not to confuse God with life. I'm no stoic. I am as upset about what happened to me as anyone could be. I feel free to curse the unfairness of life and to vent all my grief and anger. But I believe God feels the same way as I do about that accident — grieved and angry. I don't blame him for what has happened."

Douglas continued, "I have learned to see beyond the physical reality in this world to the spiritual reality. We tend to think, *Life should be fair because God is fair*. But

God is not life. If we develop a relationship with God *apart* from our life circumstances, then we may be able to hang on when the physical reality breaks down. We can learn to trust God despite all the unfairness of life."

Many biblical heroes — Abraham, Joseph, David, Elijah, Jeremiah, Daniel — went through trials much like Job's (or Douglas's). For each of them, at times, the physical reality surely seemed to present God as the enemy. But each managed to hold on to a trust in God despite the hardships. In doing so, their faith moved from a "contract faith" — I'll follow God if he treats me well — to a relationship that could transcend any hardship.

I have observed that people involved in ministry, perhaps more so than most people, live with an unstated "contract faith." After all, they're giving time and energy to work for God; don't they deserve special treatment in return?

My wife would get irritated when she got a parking ticket while stopping to pick up meat for a soup kitchen or while visiting a shut-in at the hospital. The meter expired for the very reason that she had sensed a need to devote more time to doing God's work. Her reward: a twenty-five-dollar fine and a half-day trip to the city courthouse!

Bud, one of the true "saints" in urban ministry in Chicago, nearly cut off his hand on a power saw while demonstrating to volunteers how to build houses for the homeless. What theology could possibly explain such a turn of events?

Again I go back to Douglas's phrase, "Don't confuse God with life." When doubts arise, I often turn to that great chapter by Paul, Romans 8. Many people know verse 28, "And we know that in all things God works for the good of those who love him," but my eyes jump ahead to verses later in that chapter. "Who shall separate us from the love of Christ?" asks Paul. "Shall trouble or hardship or persecution or famine or nakedness or danger or sword?" (8:35). In that one sentence, the apostle Paul summarizes his ministry autobiography. He endured all those trials for the sake of the gospel, and yet somehow he had the faith to believe that these "things"—surely not good in themselves—could nevertheless be used by God to accomplish good.

The apostle Paul had learned to see past the hardships of life to a loving God who will one day prevail. "For I am convinced that neither death nor life, neither angels nor demons, neither the present nor the future, nor any powers, neither height nor depth, nor anything else in all creation, will be able to separate us from the love of God that is in Christ Jesus our Lord," the chapter concludes triumphantly. Confidence like that can go a long way towards solving discouragement over a ministry that never quite works out the way we wish.

4) Who am I working for? If you instinctively answer a church, a pastor, or a missions committee, then you are in danger. Ministry is a "calling," and the only effective minister, whether volunteer or professional, reports to the One who called.

I have said that the true Savior had nothing of what we mistakenly call a "savior complex" today. Here is how Helmut Thielicke describes the ministry of Jesus:

> What tremendous pressures there must have been within him to drive him to hectic, nervous, explosive activity! He sees ... as no one else ever sees, with an infinite and awful nearness, the agony of the dying man, the prisoner's torment, the anguish of the wounded

conscience, injustice, terror, dread, and beastliness. He sees and hears and feels all this with the heart of a Savior.... Must not this fill every waking hour and rob him of sleep at night? Must he not begin immediately to set the fire burning, to win people, to work out strategic plans to evangelize the world, to work, work, furiously work, unceasingly, unrestingly, before the night comes when no man can work? That's what we would imagine the earthly life of the Son of God would be like, if we were to think of him in human terms.

But how utterly different was the actual life of Jesus! Though the burden of the whole world lay heavy upon his shoulders, though Corinth and Ephesus and Athens, whole continents, with all their desperate need, were dreadfully near to his heart, though suffering and sinning were going on in chamber, street corner, castle, and slums, seen only by the son of God—though this immeasurable misery and wretchedness cried aloud for a physician, he has time to stop and talk to the individual....

By being obedient in his little corner of the highly provincial precincts of Nazareth and Bethlehem he allows himself to be fitted into a great mosaic whose master is God. And that's why he has time for persons; for all time is in the hands of his Father. And that too is why peace and not unrest goes out from him. For God's faithfulness already spans the world like a rainbow: he does not need to build it; he needs only to walk beneath it. (from *The Waiting Father*)

I have visited Calcutta, India, a place of poverty, death, and irremediable human problems. There, the nuns of Mother Teresa's order serve perhaps the poorest, most miserable people on the planet: half-dead bodies whom they pick up on the streets of Calcutta. The world stands in awe at the sisters' dedication and the results of their ministry, but something about these nuns impresses me even more: their serenity. If I tackled such a mammoth, hopeless project, I would likely be scurrying about, faxing press releases to donors, begging for more resources, gulping tranquilizers, searching for ways to cope with my mounting despair. Not these nuns.

Their serenity traces back to what takes place before their day's work begins. At four o'clock in the morning, long before the sun, the sisters rise. Dressed in spotless white habits, they file into the chapel, where they pray and sing together. Before they ever meet their first "client," they have immersed themselves in worship and in the love of God.

When visitors come to the community house, the Missionaries of Charity ask them to begin their visit by praying in the chapel. Mother Teresa herself used to greet every visitor with this invitation: "Let us first greet the master of the house. Jesus is here."

I sense no panic in the sisters who run the Home for the Dying and Destitute in Calcutta. I see concern and compassion, yes, but no obsession over what did not get done. These sisters are not working to complete a caseload sheet for a social service agency. They are working for God. They begin their day with him, they end their day with him, and everything in between they present as an offering to God. God and God alone determines their worth and measures their success.

My pastor at LaSalle Street Church, Bill Leslie, used the illustration of an old hand-operated pump. He sometimes felt like such a pump, he said. Everyone who came along would reach up and pump vigorously a few times, and each time he felt something drain out of him. Finally, he was approaching a point of "burnout," when he had nothing more to give. He felt dry, desiccated.

In the midst of this period, Bill went on a week-long retreat and expressed these thoughts to his designated spiritual director, a very wise nun. He expected her to offer soothing words about what a wonderful, sacrificial person he was. Instead, she said, "Bill, there's only one thing to do if your reservoir is dry. You've got to go deeper." He realized on that retreat that for his outward journey to continue, he needed to give a higher priority to his inner journey.

In the record of Jesus' ministry on earth, I see only one time when he approached a state resembling anything like "burnout." In the Garden of Gethsemane, Jesus fell prostrate on the ground and prayed. Sweat fell from him like drops of blood. His prayers took on an uncharacteristic tone of pleading. He "offered up prayers and petitions with loud cries and tears to the one who could save him from death," Hebrews says (5:7), but of course Jesus knew he would not be saved from death. As that awareness grew inside him, Jesus felt distress. He had no community to support him—they had all fallen asleep. "Could you ... not keep watch for one hour?" he chided (Matthew 26:40).

And yet a dramatic change takes place between that scene in the Garden and all that follows. The Gospel accounts of Gethsemane show a person in distress and anguish. After Gethsemane they show a person who, more than Pilate, more than Herod, acts in utter control. Read the accounts of the trials. Jesus is no victim; he is serene, the master of his destiny.

What happened in the garden to make the difference? We have few details about the content of Jesus' prayers, for the potential witnesses were sound asleep. He may have reviewed his entire ministry on earth. The weight of all that went undone may have borne down on him: his disciples were unstable and irresponsible, the movement was at risk, the world was still home to evil and much suffering. Jesus himself seemed at the very edge of human endurance. He no more relished the idea of pain and death than you or I do.

Somehow, though, in Gethsemane Jesus worked through that crisis by transferring the burden to the Father. It was God's will he had come to do, after all, and his prayer resolved into the words, "Yet not as I will, but as you will" (26:39). Not many hours later he could cry out, in profound truth, "It is finished" (John 19:30).

I pray for that sense of detachment, of *trust*. I pray that I could see my work, my life, as an offering to God each day. I have learned that God is a God of mercy, of compassion, of grace—a trustworthy boss, to be sure. God and God alone is qualified to help me negotiate the slippery path between love for others and love for myself—a path bordered by hypersensitivity and callus.

The Sound of Trying

C. S. Lewis wrote that God "seems to do nothing of Himself which He can possibly delegate to His creatures. He commands us to do slowly and blunderingly what He could do perfectly and in the twinkling of an eye." There is no greater illustration of that principle than the church of Jesus Christ, to which God has delegated the task of embodying God's Presence in the world. All of our efforts are examples of God's delegation.

Every parent knows something of the risk of delegation, with all its joy and heartache. The child taking her very first steps holds on, then lets go, then falls, then struggles to her feet for another attempt. No one has discovered another way to learn to walk.

Yes, the church fails in its mission and makes serious blunders precisely because the church comprises human beings who will always fall short of the glory of God. That is the risk God took. Anyone who enters the church expecting perfection does not understand the nature of that risk or the nature of humanity. Just as every romantic eventually learns that marriage is the beginning, not the end, of the struggle to make love work, every Christian must learn that church is also only a beginning.

The composer Igor Stravinsky once wrote a new piece that contained a difficult violin passage. After several weeks of rehearsal the solo violinist came to Stravinsky and said that he could not play it. He had given it his best effort but found the passage too difficult, even unplayable. Stravinsky replied, "I understand that. What I am after is the sound of someone *trying* to play it." Perhaps something similar is what God had in mind with the church.

I remember hearing a similar illustration from Earl Palmer, a pastor who was defending the church against critics who dismissed it for its hypocrisy, its failures, its inability to measure up to the New Testament's high standards. Palmer, a Californian at the time, deliberately chose a community known for its cultural unsophistication.

"When the Milpitas High School orchestra attempts Beethoven's Ninth Symphony, the result is appalling," said Palmer. "I wouldn't be surprised if the performance made old Ludwig roll over in his grave despite his deafness. You might ask, 'Why bother?' Why inflict on those poor kids the terrible burden of trying to render what the immortal Beethoven had in mind? Not even the great Chicago Symphony Orchestra can attain that perfection.

"My answer is this: The Milpitas High School orchestra will give some people in that audience their only encounter with Beethoven's great Ninth Symphony. Far from perfection, it is nevertheless the only way they will hear Beethoven's message."

I remind myself of Earl Palmer's analogy whenever I start squirming in a church service. Although we may never achieve what the composer had in mind, there is no other way for those sounds to be heard on earth.

Vanishing Grace

Whatever Happened to the Good News?

Why does the church stir up such negative feelings?

Philip Yancey has been asking this all his life as a journalist. His perennial question is more relevant now than ever. Research shows that favorable opinions of Christianity have plummeted drastically—and opinions of Evangelicals have taken even deeper dives.

So what's so good about the "Good News"?

In his landmark book, *What's So Amazing about Grace*, Yancey issued a call for Christians to be as grace-filled in their behavior as they are in declaring their beliefs. He now aims this book at Christians again, showing them how they have lost respect, influence, and reputation in a newly post-Christian culture. Exploring what may have contributed to hostility toward Evangelicals—especially in their mixing of faith and politics instead of embracing more grace-filled ways of presenting the gospel—Yancey offers illuminating stories of how faith can be expressed in ways that disarm even the most cynical critics. Then he explores what is Good News and what is worth preserving in a culture that thinks it has rejected Christian faith.

Available in stores and online!

ZONDERVAN®
.com

Reaching for the Invisible God

What Can We Expect to find?

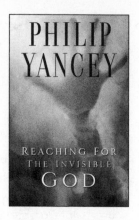

Life with God doesn't always work like we thought. High expectations slam against the reality of personal weaknesses and unwelcome surprises. And the God who we've been told longs for our company may seem remote, emotionally unavailable.

Is God playing games? What can we count on this God for?
How can we know? *How can we know God?*
This relationship with a God we can't see, hear, or touch — how does it really work?

Reaching for the Invisible God offers deep, satisfying insights that affirm and dignify the questions we're sometimes afraid to ask. Award-winning author Philip Yancey explores six foundational areas: our thirst for God, faith during times when God seems unavailable, the nature of God himself, our personal relationship with God, stages along the way, and the end goal of spiritual transformation. Honest and deeply personal, here is straight talk on Christian living for the man or woman who wants more than pat answers to life's imponderables. Ultimately, Yancey shifts the focus from our questions to the One who offers himself in answer. The God who invites us to reach for him — and find.

"I love Philip Yancey's work. He is a brilliant, graceful writer."
— Anne Lamott, author, *Traveling Mercies*

"This passionate book, unflinching in its honesty, will build your faith by helping you wrestle authentically with your doubts. Join Philip Yancey in this quest and you'll come closer still to our invisible but very real God."
— Lee Strobel, author, *The Case for Faith*

What's So Amazing About Grace?

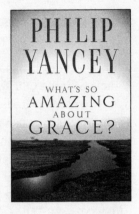

In *What's So Amazing About Grace?* award-winning author Philip Yancey explores grace at street level. If grace is God's love for the undeserving, he asks, then what does it look like in action? And if Christians are its sole dispensers, then how are we doing at lavishing grace on a world that knows far more of cruelty and unforgiveness than it does of mercy?

In his most personal and provocative book ever, Yancey offers compelling, true portraits of grace's life-changing power. He searches for its presence in his own life and in the church. And he challenges us to become living answers to a world that desperately wants to know, *What's So Amazing About Grace?*

Available in stores and online!

The Bible Jesus Read

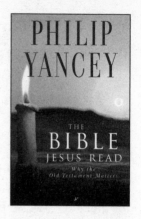

With his candid, signature style, Yancey interacts with the Old Testament from the perspective of his own deeply personal journey. From Moses, the amazing prince of Egypt, to the psalmists' turbulent emotions and the prophets' oddball rantings, Yancey paints a picture of Israel's God—and ours—that fills in the blanks of a solely New Testament vision of the Almighty.

Probing some carefully selected Old Testament books—Job, Deuteronomy, Psalms, Ecclesiastes, and the Prophets—Yancey reveals how the Old Testament deals in astonishing depths and detail with the issues that trouble us most. The Old Testament, in fact, tackles what the New Testament often only skirts. But that shouldn't surprise us. It is, after all, the Bible Jesus read.

Join Philip Yancey as he explores these sometimes shocking, often cryptic, divine writings. You will come to know God more intimately, anticipate Jesus more fervently, and find a wonderful, wise companion for your faith journey.

Available in stores and online!

The Jesus I Never Knew

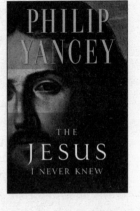

*"There is no writer in the evangelical world that
I admire and appreciate more."*
— Billy Graham

Philip Yancey helps reveal what two thousand
years of history covered up.

What happens when a respected Christian
journalist decides to put his preconceptions
aside and take a long look at the Jesus de-
scribed in the Gospels? How does the Jesus of the New Testament
compare to the "new, rediscovered" Jesus — or even the Jesus we
think we know so well?

Philip Yancey offers a new and different perspective on the life
of Christ and his work — his teachings, his miracles, his death and
resurrection — and ultimately, who he was and why he came. From
the manger in Bethlehem to the cross in Jerusalem, Yancey presents
a complex character who generates questions as well as answers; a
disturbing and exhilarating Jesus who wants to radically transform
your life and stretch your faith.

The Jesus I Never Knew uncovers a Jesus who is brilliant, creative,
challenging, fearless, compassionate, unpredictable, and ultimately
satisfying. "No one who meets Jesus ever stays the same," says
Yancey. "Jesus has rocked my own preconceptions and has made me
ask hard questions about why those of us who bear his name don't do
a better job of following him."

Where Is God When It Hurts?

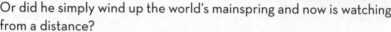

If there is a loving God, then why is it that …?

You've heard that question, perhaps asked it yourself. No matter how you complete it, at its root lies the issue of pain.

Does God order our suffering? Does he decree an abusive childhood, orchestrate a jet crash, steer a tornado through a community? Or did he simply wind up the world's mainspring and now is watching from a distance?

In this Gold Medallion Award-winning book, Philip Yancey reveals a God who is neither capricious nor unconcerned. Using examples from the Bible and from his own experiences, Yancey looks at pain — physical, emotional, and spiritual — and helps us understand why we suffer. *Where Is God When It Hurts?* will speak to those for whom life sometimes just doesn't make sense. And it will help equip anyone who wants to reach out to someone in pain but just doesn't know what to say.

Disappointment with God

Three Questions
No One Asks Aloud

Philip Yancey has a gift for articulating the knotty issues of faith. In *Disappointment with God*, he poses three questions that Christians wonder but seldom ask aloud:

- Is God unfair?
- Is he silent?
- Is he hidden?

This insightful and deeply personal book points to the odd disparity between our concept of God and the realities of life. Why, if God is so hungry for relationship with us, does he seem so distant? Why, if he cares for us, do bad things happen? What can we expect from him after all? Yancey answers these questions with clarity, richness, and biblical assurance. He takes us beyond the things that make for disillusionment to a deeper faith, a certitude of God's love, and a thirst to reach not just for what God gives, but for who he is.

Fearfully and Wonderfully Made

Mysterious, intricate, pulsing with energy ... the human body is an endlessly fascinating repository of secrets. The miracle of the skin, the strength and structure of the bones, the dynamic balance of the muscles ... your physical being is knit according to a pattern of incredible purpose. In *Fearfully and Wonderfully Made*, renowned surgeon Dr. Paul Brand and bestselling writer Philip Yancey explore the human body. Join them in a remarkable journey through inner space — a spellbinding world of cells, systems, and chemistry that bears the impress of a still deeper, unseen reality. This Gold Medallion Award-winning book uncovers eternal statements that God has made in the very structure of our bodies, presenting captivating insights into the Body of Christ.

In His Image

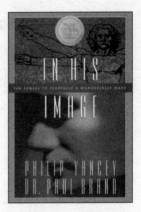

The voice of God is a heartbeat away ...

This companion book to *Fearfully and Wonderfully Made*, skillfully coauthored by award-winning writer Philip Yancey, unfolds spiritual truths through a physician's knowledge of the blood, the head, the spirit, and pain.

In *Fearfully and Wonderfully Made*, Philip Yancey and Dr. Paul Brand revealed how God's voice is encoded in the very structure of our bodies. *In His Image* takes up where its predecessor left off, beckoning us once again inward and onward to fresh exploration and discovery.

Yancey and Brand show how accurately and intricately the human body portrays the Body of Christ. In five sections — Image, Blood, Head, Spirit, and Pain — the acclaimed surgeon and the award-winning writer unlock the remarkable, living lessons contained in our physical makeup. This Gold Medallion Award-winning book will open your eyes to the complex miracle of the human body, and the even more compelling spiritual truths that it reflects.

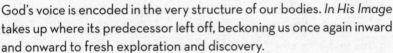

Available in stores and online!

The Gift of Pain

Why We Hurt and What We Can Do About It

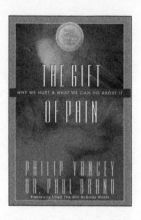

A world without pain?

Can such a place exist? It not only can —
it does. But it's no utopia. It's a colony for
leprosy patients: a world where people
literally feel no pain, and reap horrifying
consequences.

His work with leprosy patients in India and the United States convinced Dr. Paul Brand that pain truly is one of God's great gifts to us.
In this inspiring story of his fifty-year career as a healer, Dr. Brand
probes the mystery of pain and reveals its importance. As an indicator
that lets us know something is wrong, pain has a value that becomes
clearest in its absence.

The Gift of Pain looks at what pain is and why we need it. Together,
the renowned surgeon and award-winning writer Philip Yancey shed
fresh light on a gift that none of us want and none of us can do without.